THE CRAFT OF TRANSLATION

Chicago Guides
to Writing, Editing
and Publishing

On Writing, Editing, and Publishing
Essays Explicative and Hortatory
Second Edition
JACQUES BARZUN

Writing for Social Scientists
How to Start and Finish Your Thesis, Book, or Article
HOWARD S. BECKER, WITH A CHAPTER BY PAMELA RICHARDS

Chicago Guide to Preparing Electronic Manuscripts
For Authors and Publishers
PREPARED BY THE STAFF OF THE UNIVERSITY OF CHICAGO
PRESS

A Manual for Writers of Term Papers, Theses, and Dissertations
Fifth Edition
KATE TURABIAN, REVISED AND ENLARGED BY BONNIE
BIRTWISTLE HONIGSBLUM

Tales of the Field
On Writing Ethnography
JOHN VAN MAANEN

A Handbook of Biological Illustration
Second Edition
FRANCES W. ZWEIFEL

Getting into Print
The Decision-Making Process
WALTER W. POWELL

THE CRAFT OF TRANSLATION

Edited by
JOHN BIGUENET
and
RAINER SCHULTE

THE UNIVERSITY OF CHICAGO PRESS
CHICAGO AND LONDON

JOHN BIGUENET, past president of the American Literary
Translators Association, is professor of English at Loyola
University in New Orleans.

RAINER SCHULTE is professor of arts and humanities and
director of the Center for Translation Studies at the University
of Texas at Dallas and editor of *Translation Review.*

The University of Chicago Press, Chicago 60637
The University of Chicago Press, Ltd., London
© 1989 by The University of Chicago
All rights reserved. Published 1989
Printed in the United States of America

98 97 96 95 94 93 92 91 90 89   54321

Library of Congress Cataloging-in-Publication Data
The Craft of translation / edited by John Biguenet and Rainer Schulte.
    p.   cm.—(Chicago guides to writing, editing, and
publishing)
        ISBN 0-226-04868-3.—ISBN 0-226-04869-1 (pbk.)
        1. Translating and interpreting. I. Biguenet, John.
    II. Schulte, Rainer, 1937– . III. Series.
    P306.C73   1989
418'.02—dc19   88-33600
                                                          CIP

⊗ The paper used in this publication meets
the minimum requirements of the American
National Standard for Information
Sciences—Permanence of Paper for Printed
Library Materials, ANSI Z39.48–1984.

CONTENTS

INTRODUCTION

The essays included in this volume deal with the reconstruction of the translation process. Practicing translators provide insights into the complex and at times frustrating process of transferring situations from a source language text into English. The texts they have translated are literary works from both the Western and the Eastern worlds. Naturally, each language poses its own problems, but the practical considerations that go into the making of a translation do not seem to differ much from one translator to the next. All translators agree that the perfect translation remains an impossibility. Gregory Rabassa gives expression to that recognition when he writes: "a translation can never equal the original; it can approach it, and its quality can only be judged as to accuracy by how close it gets."

The essays comprise a variety of aspects that provide the reader with insights into the complex process of recreating a source-language text in English. Christopher Middleton and William Weaver retrace every step that the translator has to undertake from the first reading of the text to the final polished draft of the text's translation. Weaver illustrates the process by translating the opening paragraph of a novel by the Italian writer Carlo Emilio Gadda, and Middleton pursues the interpretive problems that are inherent in translating a specific poem by the German poet Günter Eich. The record of the steps that go into the making of these translations opens the reader's eyes to the fascinating intricacies of the translator's craft.

Margaret Sayers Peden reconstructs the architecture of a sonnet by Sor Juana Inés de la Cruz; her interpretive vision of that poem is enlarged through a juxtaposition of nine different translations of the poem, including her own. John Felstiner is also very much concerned with the reading activity that precedes any translation: "The fullest reading of a poem gets realized moment by moment in the writing of a poem. So translation presents not merely a paradigm but the utmost case of engaged literary interpretation." He has chosen to demonstrate this process by reconstructing the multiple linguistic, cultural, and historical forces that went into the creation of Paul Celan's poem "Nah, im Aortenbogen." Only after the translator has undertaken a thorough exploration of the personal and cultural layers that interact in this poem can he engage in a successful translation. Edmund Keeley explores the positive and negative points of collaborative translations by reflecting on his own collaboration with various authors and translators. Donald Frame's concern centers on the reconstruction of a writer's tone and how he tried to do justice to the tone of such writers as Molière and Rabelais. Burton Raffel introduces considerations about the translation of medieval texts, texts that by their content, linguistic features, and cultural context are quite removed from contemporary ways of seeing and writing. Edward Seidensticker explores the difficulties and impossibilities of transplanting texts from an Eastern language (in his case Japanese) into the linguistic structures of a Western language. Any literal translation from Japanese into English is not really possible, because of vast language differences in semantic connotations and grammatical structures. And Gregory Rabassa once again underlines the precariousness of the translator's undertaking. A translation can never equal the original, since the word is a metaphor for the object. Many variants complicate the translator's task: connotations vary according to the magnetic field of words in other languages and according to the reader's experience. Translation can be called an act of "transformation" that adapts a new metaphor to the original metaphor. Thus, translation is a process of choice and, consequently, never a finished process.

In these essays, the translators have focused their attention on the sequence of decisions that constitute translation. As they investigate the workings that underlie the practice of translation, it becomes more and more evident that the reconstruction of the translation process leads to the formulation of methods that are fundamental not only to the practice of translation but also to the act of reading and interpreting. In different ways, similar concepts about the nature of the craft of translation emerge from their essays, concepts that are in the making and therefore have not yet reached clearly defined directions and resolutions. These essays are dialogues between the translators and the texts with which they come in contact, and through that interaction the translators begin to formulate concepts about the nature of the craft of translation. They all echo Gregory Rabassa's assessment of the translation process: "It is my feeling that a translation is never finished, that it is open and could go on to infinity. . . . Translation is a disturbing craft because there is precious little certainty about what we are doing, which makes it so difficult in this age of fervent belief and ideology, this age of greed and screed." Even though this sense of uncertainty haunts every translator, the topics and concerns discussed in these essays are strikingly similar in tone and perception. Certain questions continuously weigh upon the minds of these translators: What kind of interpretive reading must the translator engage in to do justice to a text before the actual translation can take place? How can equivalencies be established between the semantic and cultural differences of two languages? What constitutes a successful translation?

All acts of translation begin with a thorough investigation of the reading process. Translators, by necessity, read each word and sentence at least as carefully as the critic or the scholar. Even the smallest detail in a text, as Rabassa points out, cannot be neglected. Therefore, it is no coincidence that almost all translators presented in this volume address the question of reading. Peden informs the reader that a more serious title for her essay would be: "Reading Poem 145 of Sor Juana Inés de la Cruz: Variations on a Sonnet." William Weaver thinks through every linguistic and cultural nuance of each word in the opening paragraph of Gadda's novel. Felstiner and Middleton undertake similar detailed readings of each word in the poems they plan to translate. They explore each word first as word and then as a reflection of a larger cultural and historical context. Studying the working methods of these translators enables the reader to participate in the ever expanding associations and layers of meaning that are inherent in complex literary works.

The philosopher Hans Georg Gadamer in his work "To What Extent Does Language Prescribe Thinking?" succinctly expresses the relationship between reading and translating: "Reading is already translation, and translation is translation for the second time. . . . The process of translating comprises in its essence the whole secret of human understanding of the world and of social communication." Gadamer confirms one of the basic assumptions of translation studies, that all acts of communication are acts of translation.

In contrast to the critical inquiry of a text, which frequently assesses, describes, and evaluates the implications of content in a work, the translator/reader focuses on the word and sentence as process, as possibilities toward meanings. Although criticism and scholarship might already have surrounded a work by fixed opinions of interpretation, translators always have to rethink the web of interrelationships in a text before any translation becomes feasible.

"Reading is already *translation*." Through the process of reading, readers are transplanted into the atmosphere of a new situation
that does not build just one clearly defined reality, but rather possibilities of various realities. Reading reestablishes the uncertainty
of the word, both as isolated phenomenon and as semantic possibility of a sentence, paragraph, or the context of the entire work.
The rediscovery of that uncertainty in each word constitutes the
initial attitude of the translator. Reading becomes the making of
meaning and not the description of already fixed meanings. The
imaginative literary text places the reader between several realities
that need to be deciphered and adjusted to the specific perspectives
of seeing that the reader brings to the text. The act of reading
should be seen as the generator of uncertainties, as the driving
force toward a decision-making process, as the discovery of new
interrelations that can be experienced but not described in terms of
a content-oriented language. In the translation process there are no
definitive answers, only attempts at solutions in response to states
of uncertainty generated by the interaction of the words' semantic
fields and sounds. Reading promotes the making of meanings
through questions in which the possibility of an answer results in
another question: What if?

Reading transforms the text, and in transplanting the text into
the environment of a new language, the translator continues that
process of transformation. Without transformation there is no
translation; perhaps that is the reason why literal translations have
never been successful in the transferral of works of literature. William Weaver echoes this uncertainty when he writes: "The worst
mistake a translator can commit is to reassure himself by saying
'that's what it says in the original,' and renouncing the struggle to
do his best. The words of the original are only the starting point;
a translator must do more than convey information (a literary
translator, that is)."

Words, however, initiate the reading and interpretive process
that ultimately leads to the act of translation. Translators, in their
act of reading, interact in a particular way with words. They reex-
amine words with respect to their semantic and cultural functions.
Gregory Rabassa describes the intensity with which a translator
approaches a text: "I have always maintained that translation is essentially the closest reading one can possibly give a text. The translator cannot ignore 'lesser' words, but must consider every jot and
tittle."

The presence of the word emerges first as a semantic field with its own tradition, and then as a changing entity in the construction of meanings within a given text. Words have the potential of expanding the boundaries of their lexical meanings and the dynamics of semantic possibilities through their specific contextual placement. Henry James, in his story "The Beast in the Jungle," repeatedly uses the word "to know." The word carries with it a previously defined lexical meaning; this meaning, however, is of little use in a serious attempt at interpreting James's story. Each time the word appears in the story, it takes on an expanded meaning generated by the contextual progression of the text. At times, the meanings these words project are difficult to capture within the possibilities of descriptive critical language, and they certainly transcend the limitations of dictionary definitions. Their effect can be determined only in their contextual environment. Therefore, translators must develop modes of thinking that reconnect them with the dynamic fields of words, modes of thinking that will allow them to explore meaning associations within a word and meaning connections created by words in a specific context.

The reconstruction process of the linguistic and cultural implications raises the question of the "literal" translation. It is a generally accepted fact that literal translations cannot be successful with literary works. At the beginning of his essay, Edward Seidensticker demonstrates what levels of noncommunication can be reached when translators try to carry meanings across from Japanese into English by employing a literal technique of translation. The literal translation focuses on the word as word without considering the larger realm of the context of the work and its placement within a cultural and historical frame. The reconstruction of the translation process reveals that words always point beyond themselves in a literary text. Furthermore, all literary works are fragments—as are perhaps all artistic creations—and translators have to take it upon themselves to reconstruct the total image and situation that is conveyed through the limiting possibilities of language. Literal translation deals with the surface appearance of words without a reflection of the directions of meaning that the original author tried to materialize behind that surface. The reader of such a translation will be confused and will experience great difficulties in visualizing the situations of the original text and its relationships to subsequent expansions of such situations.

Translations must reproduce the whole by trying to put the

particulars of a text into focus and interaction. The act of reconstruction, that probing of what reality there is behind the surface
of the words used on the page, is *the* act of interpretation. By re-
tracing the steps that underlie any act of interpretation through the
eyes of the translator's meticulous work, the reader recognizes that
situational or pictorial thinking is the foundation of all interpretation. It is first the pictorial visualization that goes with one word
and then the interaction that a word establishes with the rest of a
sentence or a passage. Translators must balance the individual word
with the whole of a work. Through this practice of constantly bal-
ancing the dynamics of words in one place with other moments in
the text, the translator demonstrates how associative and contextual
thinking comes about. Translators cannot approach the text from a
linear point of view; they must be present simultaneously at various
points of a text.

The "word itself" becomes a creative power to explore new
ways of meaning. In that respect, the translation process affirms the
"how" and not the "what" of reading and understanding. If one
asks the question, "what does something mean," one expects a
statementlike answer. If one asks, "how does something come to
mean," avenues are opened that lead to the exploration of the complexities inherent in a text, thereby creating the possibility of arriving at more than one response to the text. Translators, in their attempts to interpret, shy away from reducing texts to simple
statements of interpretation. Rather, the translator's efforts are directed toward the discovery of relationships in a text: relationships
between words, relationships between the word and its philological
and etymological background, relationships between the word and
its cultural ambiance, relationships between the word and its historical tradition, relationships between the word and its context
within a text.

Translation activities are anchored in "situational" thinking.
Translation revitalizes the thought process by thinking out possibilities of interaction and meaning within a given text, to choose
from these possibilities a solution that comes close to the atmosphere of the situation. In the translation process, thinking grows
out of the situation within a text; it is not brought to the text from
the outside.

The translator will always reconnect us, the readers, scholars, and
critics, with the function of the word as an isolated phenomenon

and as a means of building a contextual situation of meanings and emotions.

The activity of the translator starts with the reality of the word on the page. It is common knowledge that no language has created enough words to express all the nuances of our emotional and intellectual existence. Some languages are richer than others in their word count; some languages are richer in sound quality than others. The atmosphere that a romance language creates through the sounds of words might have to be recreated in English through other linguistic possibilities. An exact equivalence from one language to another will never be possible. This could be characterized as both the dilemma and the challenge for the translator. Not even on the level of individual words—either within the same language or from one language to the next—can exact equivalencies be found. No two synonyms are quite the same, which makes room for a certain area of ambiguity within a language and therefore opens it up for genuine communication, since meaningful communication has to go beyond the level of descriptive, logical statements within any language.

The translator's first and foremost concern, then, must be the continuous involvement in experiencing and defining the boundaries of meanings and associations surrounding each word. That activity has to happen both in the source language and in English. One could say that the translator draws a visual image of each word that evolves into a painting whose outer edges can never be clearly defined. In those moments, one word begins to flow into the colors of the next. This activity will also reveal that some words have a larger field of connotations than the corresponding word in another language. The English words "clock" and "watch" shrink into one word in German: *die Uhr*. The transferral from English into German thus poses fewer problems than the reverse: when translators encounter the word in a German text, they have to visualize the situation in the source-language text to decide whether it should be transplanted as "watch" or "clock." Rabassa demonstrates this phenomenon with the translation of the Spanish word *rama*. He says: "If translated as 'branch,' it can be applied equally to a tree or a bank (fiscal variety), both of which meanings obtain in both languages. If we were to translate 'rama' as 'limb,' however, perfectly legitimate if it belongs to a tree, we have brought into our English version the nuance of an arm or a leg, something the Spanish word does not contain, and then there is 'bough,' which can be applied neither to a bank nor to a human appendage." At all times, the translator has to assess the boundaries of these words and the situations they create within a text; what he or she discovers is not only the sameness of meanings inherent in two words, but also the refined differences. That exploration of the differences constitutes one of the most essential contributions of the translator as a mediator between the surface appearance of a word and its semantic, etymological, and cultural weight. The practice of that activity also reconnects the reader with the power of individual words and how these words come to express meanings within the context of a particular text.

The reality of nonequivalencies among words can be extended to situations in different cultures. Human emotions hardly change from one culture to another; what changes is the way one perceives these emotions and how one places them within the natural environment of a country. A word approximates its synonym without ever replacing it. A cultural situation—whether in the realm of social, ethical, educational, legal, or political realities—never finds its exact equivalent in another country. Here again, translators must assess the boundaries of every individual cultural situation to define both the sameness and the differences. As in the case of words, the comparative study of cultural situations will prominently display the different ways in which we perceive and create our cultural reality. And in that sense, the translator's methodologies introduce the readers into the complexities of cultural thinking and expressions rather than reducing these complexities to a common denominator.

Mention needs to be made of the translator's own perspective, which precedes any kind of interpretation. Words don't find their equivalencies in the new language, nor do cultural expressions, and the translator will never approach a text twice the same way. Both Rabassa and Weaver use the same example to illustrate this point. On one day the translator might say "maybe" and on the next day "perhaps" for the same word in the source-language text. That dimension of the reading process has received some attention in critical and scholarly writing during the last few years. How do readers interact with a text and how do translators formulate their perspectives of seeing and interpreting when they first come in contact with a literary work? Since very little documentation exists on how the reader reacts to a text, it might be appropriate once again to look at the translator's approach to a text in order to extract some understanding about the concept of "perspectives" in the act of translation. One of the most fruitful areas of investigation can be identified in the study of multiple translations: the same text translated by more than one translator. We know that two different translators will never come up with exactly the same translation, since their initial way of seeing a work varies according to the presuppositions they bring to a text. No two translators perceive every moment in a text with a similar awareness or intensity, which leads to varying value judgments within a text about what elements should be chiseled out for the act of transplantation from the source-language situation into the target language.

To place this rather delicate interpretive process into a practical context, it might be helpful to look at the first line of Rainer Maria Rilke's well-known poem "The Panther." The differences of perception and interpretive judgments are evident in the very first line of the poem. The German line reads: "Sein Blick ist vom Vorübergehen der Stäbe so müd geworden. . . ." This line has been rendered by several translators in the following ways:

"His gaze, from sweeping by the bars, has worn so thin. . . ."
    (John Felstiner)
"From seeing the bars, his seeing is so exhausted. . . ." (Robert Bly)
"His sight, from glancing back and forth across the bars. . . ."
    (James L. Dana)
"His sight from ever gazing through the bars. . . ."
    (C. F. MacIntyre)
"The bars have sucked his glance so dry of raging. . . ."
    (Ludwig Lewisohn)
"His vision from the passing of the bars is grown so weary. . . ."
    (M. D. Herter Norton)

Each one of these translators has taken a different approach to the interpretation of the first line of the poem. Linguistically speaking, no two are the same. As a matter of fact, a comparative evaluation of these lines shows that they are quite different in their intensity of perception. However, only one of the translators has chosen to maintain the situation of the original in his translation. Herter Norton captures the unusual distortion in the first line: it is not the eyes of the panther that are moving; rather, that movement has been transferred to the bars of the cage. The bars move, which might be interpreted as a particular poetic device conceived by Rilke. It would be of interest to the study of the translation process to find out whether all the other translators ignored that nuance, whether they failed to see it in the original German, or whether they felt that it was not important enough for their overall interpretive view of the poem. The juxtaposition of these translations, however, conveys an intriguing insight into the translation process and shows how different perceptions or angles of approach shape the overall direction of a translation. The next step of a comparative examination of these translations should address how consistent each translator was in his translation once a perspective had been established.

The previous remarks begin to uncover the tremendously intricate mental procedures that translators must undertake in order to gain interpretive insights into literary texts. Only after translators have enacted the various steps of placing words in their semantic and cultural contexts can they hope to engage in the successful transplantation of situations from another culture into English. Burton Raffel gives succinct expression to the enormous responsibility that translators face in their conscientious efforts to communicate perspectives of world views across language boundaries when he writes toward the end of his essay that "the literary translator is necessarily engaged with far more than words, far more than techniques, far more than stories or characters or scenes. He is engaged with world views, and with the passionately held inner convictions of men and women. . . . A large part of his task, and perhaps the most interesting . . . is the mining out and reconstruction of those world views, those passionately held and beautifully embodied inner convictions." The following essays show how each translator struggled with the transplantation of words through which human emotions and passions become reality.

NO TWO SNOWFLAKES ARE ALIKE: TRANSLATION AS METAPHOR

GREGORY RABASSA

Wishful thinking and early training in arithmetic have convinced a majority of people that there are such things as equals in the world. A more severe examination of comparisons, however, will quickly show us that all objects, alive or otherwise, are thoroughly individual in spite of close resemblances. Schooled as we are from the time of our first letters and figures in such things as $2 = 2$, we rarely wake up to the fact that this is impossible, except as a purely theoretical and fanciful concept, for the second 2 is obviously a hair younger than the first and therefore not its equal. With this in mind, we should certainly not expect that a word in one language will find its equal in another. Indeed, mathematicians today are more cautious than their forebears and more often than not say "approaches" rather than "equals." In this sense, then, a translation can never equal the original; it can approach it, and its quality can only be judged as to accuracy by how close it gets.

A word is nothing but a metaphor for an object or, in some cases, for another word. This aspect of language is admirably shown in the third part of *Gulliver's Travels,* where Dean Swift describes a "project" at the school of languages in the Academy of Lagado, whereby, in order to do away with the bothersome intermediary of words, people will avail themselves of the objects in question, carried in a sack and brought out when the thing otherwise would have been named, thus avoiding the necessity of words and the dangerous nuances entailed therein. Following this notion of Swift's, then, we can see that a word in translation is at two removes from the object under description. The word "dog" and the word *perro* may conjure up a like image in the mind of the Englishman and the mind of the Spaniard, but other subliminal images may accompany the two versions and thereby give the two words further differences beyond sound; the Portuguese word *cão* is closer to the Latin root that gives us "canine," opening up our minds to broader connotations.

Following the example above and showing that, like words, no

Gregory Rabassa is distinguished professor of Romance languages at Queens College and the Graduate School, City University of New York. He has translated works by Julio Cortázar, Clarice Lispector, Mario Vargas Llosa, Juan Goytisolo, Miguel Angel Asturias, Demetrio Aguilera-Malta, and Gabriel García Márquez.

two metaphors are alike regardless of similarity, we can take the case of the reader's past experience with dogs: one may have had a delightful pet in childhood and, therefore, is warmed by the word as he comes across it, while another may have been bitten by a vicious cur at the same period in life and will get a chill or a feeling of fright. Continuing on doggedly, we must also take cultural differences into account. Among some peoples, Muslims, for example, the dog is considered a vile creature, worthy of a swift kick, while others, notably those of northern Europe, dote on him. So that "dog" can never translate *perro* in all of its hidden senses. A more succinct example is the fact that cocks do not crow alike in the ears of different peoples: an American rooster sings "cock-a-doodle-doo," but carry him to Mexico and he will say *qui-qui-ri-qui*.

In light of the above, then, translation is really what we might call transformation. It is a form of adaptation, making the new metaphor fit the original metaphor, and in a bad translation the results can be most procrustean. Jorge Luis Borges had a fine sense of how words are used and of their Swiftian limitations when he told his translator not to write what he said but what he wanted to say. In this case Borges was taking advantage of a Spanish idiom in order to produce (if we may approach his terminology) a bifurcated sense: the expression *quiero decir* in Spanish literally means "I want to say" (sometimes carried to "I am trying to say"), but it has come to have the idiomatic sense of *I mean*. What the Argentinian author was doing was stressing the inadequacy of words as we strive for some platonical form of expression that would be more practical than the Lagadian solution. Looking at the English equivalent of *quiero decir*, "I mean," we must remember how often we use just that phrase to correct or reword what we are "trying to say" ("What I mean is . . . ," etc.).

More deadly even than personal and cultural nuances in hindering an "exact" translation is the very sound of languages and the words that constitute them. We have already seen how the crow of the cock differs, so it is quite natural that the names of objects should receive varying sounds. This makes for extreme difficulty in the translation of poetry, as might be imagined, especially when rhyme is involved. The rooster has shown us that onomatopoeia varies from tongue to tongue, and authors will marshal the very sounds of their language in order to squeeze out its ultimate effects. Shakespeare says, "A drum! a drum! Macbeth doth come," but this thunderous announcement would bumble along in French as "Un tambour! un tambour! Macbeth vient." It is obvious that the translator will have to take liberties with the text in order to preserve the spirit of what Shakespeare "wants to say." The other side of the coin is seen (or heard) when Verlaine organizes the sounds peculiar to the French language to imitate the wail of a violin (it sounds more like a cello to me) as he says, "Les sanglots longs des violons de l'automne." English simply has no matching nasal sounds in words that would convey the meaning, unless we turn to trombones, and then we have changed instruments, although that may be more in keeping with what translation is all about.

Words and phrases, then, are not just descriptions of the objects or circumstances entailed, but more often than not denote the spirit involved. Almost as difficult as poetry to render into another language are curses and oaths. The meanings can be quite different, but the spirit is universally human enough to be the same. Therefore, when we translate a curse, we must look to the feelings behind it and not the words that go to make it up. In English, when we insult someone's maternal descent, we call the person a "*son of a bitch*," while in Spanish he is an *hijo de puta*, "son of a whore." The closest in English to this latter is the archaic "whoreson," which, even if understood, would not arouse much more than a ripple of indignation. Portuguese leaves it up to the listener's imagination to deduce the impact by simply saying *filho da mãe*, "son of your mother," which is patent and obvious, but leaves the door open to all manner of vile conjectures regarding one's dam. A most common insult in Spanish is *cabrón*, "cuckold." There is no really exact equivalent in English, for the word itself would be about as effective as "whoreson." Indeed, many people would not know what you were talking about.

It should also be noted that Spanish is completely different from English in the way it arrives at the term for the hapless husband. English goes to the European cuckoo, who lays its eggs in other birds' nests (the American does no such thing; here the culprit is the cowbird), while Spanish resorts to the image of the billy goat. There is irony behind this epithet as the goat has traditionally been the symbol of male sexuality, as portrayed in the figure of satyrs and other creatures. Thus the sex victim is derisively called by the name of the one who has wronged him. This is in the same spirit as the word *dunce*, derived from the name of Duns Scotus, reputed to be the wisest man of his day, or akin to the way we call

the village dimwit Einstein. This whole concept makes it difficult
to render into English the numerous conceits found in Mediterra-
nean literature and folklore having to do with horns. Saint Jerome
should have been more alert to the consequences when he nodded
in his translation of the Hebrew of the Old Testament and led Mi-
chelangelo to give his Moses a pair of horns for all to see.

In Genesis, Adam is given the delightful privilege of naming
the newly created animals. This was also the inventive chore of the
discoverers and explorers of the New World when they came upon
flora and fauna unknown to their philosophies. The Mexican writer
Andrés Iduarte used to say that he wanted to be the first person on
the moon simply to be able to name things. The newcomers had
recourse to three different methods in their nomenclature: they
could accept the Indian name, in a version usually colored by their
own tongue; they could assign a name that identified the creature
as one approaching a known animal in the Old World; or they
could apply an entirely new and descriptive name to the being. We
have many examples of all three methods. Woodchuck, quetzal, and
jaguar are examples of the first, but some Spaniards, when they
spied the last for the first time, baptized it *tigre,* even though they
had never been to India or seen a tiger. The Portuguese, who had
been there, were more accurate, calling it *onça* (ounce). The American robin, sometimes pedantically and more accurately called mi-
gratory thrush, a translation of its Latin scientific name (*turdus
migratorius*), which can be counted on to set schoolboys a-
giggling, is really quite different from the European variety. Examples of descriptive names would be prairie dog and armadillo.

We are what we are called, to such a degree that ever so many
adjectives have been coined from proper names, for example, *Chur-
chillian, cervantino, balzacien.* Without a name we have no identity.
Sometimes a name is what gives an object existence. Bill Klem, for
many years dean of National League umpires, eloquently described
his position as creator through nomenclature when he said, "It ain't
nothin' till I say what it is. It ain't a ball, it ain't a strike, it ain't
nothin'." In these cases of linguistic creation the translator must
recreate and he must do so wisely and with extreme care. He must
know that *tigre* can mean "tiger" in English only when the creature
is a denizen of the Old World. When a *tigre* turns up in Venezuela,
it must perforce be rendered as "jaguar" for the sake of accuracy
and at the expense of all the connotations carried in the original
misnaming on the part of the discoverers. Somehow the Venezue-

lan dictum, "Donde ronca tigre, no hay burro con reumatismo" (Where the jaguar growls there are no donkeys with rheumatism) would lose its strength if we substituted *jaguar* for *tigre* in Spanish, yet that is what we must do in English. The result is as flat as substituting "groundhog" for "woodchuck" in "How much wood could a woodchuck chuck if a woodchuck could chuck wood," or akin to what happened to the name of the brokerage house when Mr. Bean was replaced by Mr. Smith: Merrill, Lynch, Pierce, Fenner, and Bean went out of tune on its last note when it became Merrill, Lynch, Pierce, Fenner, and Smith. Somebody hit a black key.

There are nuances of meaning that sometimes lurk in differing titles for the same creature or object. In English, "vulture" and "buzzard" are words that describe the same bird, but when these names are turned into epithets and applied to human beings, they are quite different: an "old buzzard" is quite another thing from an "old vulture." The first connotes foolish senility, the second rapacity. In Portuguese there is a subtle difference between *burrice* and *asneira*, activities ascribed to humans as they are compared to a *burro* or an *asno*, two different ways of saying donkey. In English, there is a slight difference in tone if we call a person an "ass" or a "jackass" (the jenny seems to have escaped any stigma in this one). In American usage, with the confusion between "ass" and "arse," the term "asshole" (which Julio Cortázar loved because it had no real equivalent in Spanish) seems to carry more of the spirit of the beast of burden rather than the anal orifice. Even the English, who normally keep the two terms apart by proper pronunciation, often adopt the American way in this instance.

In speech and in writing what we do essentially is choose the word (or metaphor) that we think, sometimes instinctively, best describes or conveys the meaning of what we want to communicate (Borges again). The author makes his or her choice and puts it down in writing. Along comes the translator, who must then make another choice, but in a different language and on a different level. Sometimes the *one* possible word in the original is faced by several possible translations in the second language (I eschew "target language" because when I was in the infantry a target was something to shoot at and, ideally, kill, which does, indeed, often happen in the matter of translation). What could be set forth as a classic example between Spanish and English is the word *rama*. If translated as "branch," it can be applied equally to a tree or a bank (fiscal variety), both of which meanings obtain in both languages. If we are to translate *rama* as "limb," however, perfectly legitimate if it belongs to a tree, we have brought into our English version the nuance of an arm or a leg, something the Spanish word does not contain, and then there is "bough," which can be applied neither to a bank nor to a human appendage. This would bring on unwanted ramifications if the Spanish translator is called upon to translate the line from the nursery rhyme, "When the bough breaks."

It is this matter of choice that bedevils the translator as he seeks to approach the language he is working from as closely as possible. In certain cases it comes down to such elemental things as articles. I have always maintained that translation is essentially the closest reading one can possibly give a text. The translator cannot ignore "lesser" words, but must consider every jot and tittle. In the case cf Latin and Russian, for example, there are no articles. Bringing them into English and many other languages, the translator must decide what the author "wanted to say." Is it "the dog" or "a dog?" The important difference between the two concepts (as far as we who work in English are concerned) was left to the unspoken imagination of the Romans.

In most works of literature the opening line is normally a very pithy one, giving all kinds of directions and definitions to the work as a whole. Those of us who did Latin in high school with Miss Whitford had to commit to memory those first ten lines of the *Aeneid* that start out with "Arma virumque cano" (without long marks, a sign of our new exalted status as we left Cicero behind). The standard classroom version, backed up by any number of ponies, was "I sing of arms and the man. . . ." Rolfe Humphries says, "Arms and the man I sing"; Shaw uses it for the title of a play. Then some years later, along came Allen Mandelbaum ("I sing of arms and of a man") and Robert Fitzgerald ("I sing of warfare and a man at war"), using the indefinite article instead of the traditional definite one. The meaning is clearly different in these two differing choices. In the one case, Aeneas would seem to be *the* man, the one anointed by the gods for his sacred mission to refound Troy as Rome, while in the other he is *a* man who happened to be picked by fate to fulfill that high endeavor. Both versions make sense, but the discrepancy is obvious. If we accept one or the other, we are making two quite different choices as to the interpretation of Aeneas's position. Is he a demigod (his mother *is* Venus) above all other men, or is he more human, Everyman, chosen by lot for this noble destiny? Unfortunately, unlike Borges, Virgil was not around to tell his translators what he meant or wanted to say. Neither do we have any explanations from his contemporaries. We can only be envious of his Russian translators, who can follow right along without any article problem and not be faced with the difficulties incumbent upon two different poems.

All of this shows us that the process of translation is one of choice. The skill of the translator lies in the use of instinct or, better, what Ortega y Gasset calls "vital reason," using Alexander's actions at Gordia as an example of how it works, a kind of acquired instinct, much the way we put on the brakes when a dog dashes in front of our car. This necessarily human part of choice is illustrated by the often cited report of what a computer in Japan did when it attempted to translate the phrase "Out of sight, out of mind," coming up with the perfectly logical meaning of "Confined to an insane asylum." As we have said before, however, the past experience of the individual will affect the translator in the same way that it does the reader. People have a kind of liking for certain words, either from experience and background or by cultivated preference, as exemplified by the vocabulary of W. C. Fields. This becomes evident as we find ourselves having to rewrite what we have done because we have favored some words too much. There might even be some atmospheric influence, for I have found myself using a word on Monday and then changing it to something else on Tuesday, only to go back to the original choice on Wednesday. This might be the influence of academe, as those of us who teach have become accustomed to living by MWF and TuThS (although the S has been long gone for some time now). Perhaps there are MWF words and TuThS words, with our minds resting and going blank on Sunday.

These incessant changes are the bugbear of the translator. It is my feeling that a translation is never finished, that it is open and could go on to infinity, like the figure on the old box of Aunt Jemima pancake flour (Aunt Jemima holds a box that shows Aunt Jemima holding a box that shows Aunt Jemima holding a box . . .). The phenomenon in question is doubtless because the choices made in translation are never as secure as those made by the author. Since we are not writing our own material, we are still unsure whether or not the word we have used is the best one, either for meaning or for sound or for ever so many other reasons. I am always distressed when I receive the usually handsome copy of a book I have translated. I like the dust jacket most of the time and if it is by Knopf the description at the end of the type used, because when I start to read the thing, on page one already, I start having second thoughts about word choice and how it would have been so much better had I said this instead of that. I rarely read these through, only when I must use one as a textbook, because it is simply too upsetting to run across so many "should-have-beens." Rationally, however, there is really nothing wrong with the translation and any number of reviewers have allowed so, but that old matter of the proper choice remains and I am dissatisfied. It is this feeling possibly that lies beneath the need for new translations of old books every so often while the original text goes on and on in all its glory.

George Steiner speaks of this in his masterful *After Babel* and Jorge Luis Borges illustrates the matter in his *ficción* entitled "Pierre Menard, Author of the *Quijote*." The fact is that there is a kind of continental drift that slowly works on language as words wander away from their original spot in the lexicon and suffer the accretion of subtle new nuances, which, as the authors mentioned above demonstrate, result from distortions brought about by time and the events that people it. The choice made by an earlier translator, then, no longer obtains and we must choose again. Through some instinct wrought of genius, the author's original choices of word and idiom seem to endure. This is in line with my dissatisfaction with what I have translated, as I mentioned above. When something of my own finally comes out in print, I am most often rather pleased with it, and I rarely see any need for emendation. The passage of time has removed me from the sense that this is my work, and it seems to be that of someone else. In the case of my own stuff, I feel that this fellow has done quite well here, this is just the way I would have put it, while in the case of translation I wonder why the boob said it this way when it would have been so much better put another way. Perhaps literary translation should be a continuous process, what the jargon calls "on-going," a labor of Sisyphus, as it were.

The author who knows his language inside out can be either the easiest or the hardest to translate. If he has what might be termed a classical style or use of language, that is, if his sense of words is so pure that as metaphors they approach the object portrayed most closely, the translator is on his mettle to find that same closely approaching word in his language. A writer like Gabriel García Márquez has this gift of language, and he is so exact in his choice of words, getting ever so close to what he wants to say, that, indeed, it is difficult to make a botch of a translation of his work as he leads you along to a similar closeness in English of metaphor (word) and object.

My most amazing experience along these lines, being led by the author, occurred, however, with quite a different kind of writer, one who was most difficult to translate for the same reason that he knew his language so well, the Cuban poet and novelist José Lezama Lima. As I worked away at the arduous but rewarding task of rendering his novel *Paradiso* into English, I came upon a few lines from two American poets that Lezama had translated into Spanish, Walt Whitman and Hart Crane. At the moment I did not have a text of the originals at hand and in order to facilitate the process of translation I rendered the lines back into English. When I finally did get hold of the original versions I found that I had missed by only a couple of words in both cases. I attribute this result to the fact that Lezama Lima had made such a perfect translation of the poets that I would inexorably and of needs have to arrive at a version quite close to the original. Would that everything I did could have turned out so close.

In most cases Lezama offered more difficult challenges. Like James Joyce, he had such a grasp of the language that he could see beyond its confines and, since his mind was broader than the language, went about inventing neologisms and restructuring the tongue in quite a logical way so as to express thoughts and feelings that lay beyond the norms of its expression. The translator is thereby put to the test to expand his own language in order to match what the original is saying. Sometimes, however, he will find that his language does have an expression or turn of phrase or construction that fills the gap that the adventurous author is trying to take care of in his language. The problem for the translator here is that his version will be commonplace and will not show the author's newly coined discovery. Therefore he must lay his standard translation aside and seek something new that will both give the meaning of what the author wants to say and make it quite clear that something new has been added to both languages.

This close knowledge of the language works in an inward fashion as well, and there, too, it defies the skills of the translator. I know of an outstanding example and one that I really think impossible to render into any other language. It is the epigraph that follows the title of the Brazilian João Guimarães Rosa's novel *Grande Sertão: Veredas* (absurdly translated into English as *The Devil to Pay in the Backlands,* although I don't know what else could have been done with it). The epigraph states, "O diabo na rua no meio do redemoinho" (The devil in the street in the middle of the whirlwind).

Rosa has put the devil not only in the middle of the whirlwind in the street but also in the very word for whirlwind: *re-demoinho;* one of the words for devil (demon) in Portuguese is *demo,* and there he is in the middle of the word as well. Thomas Colchie has received a Guggenheim grant to produce a new and proper version of this great novel and I do not envy him as he faces this particular problem.

Another aspect of a deep knowledge of one's own language is a thoroughgoing familiarity with local expression and idiom on the part of an author. In many cases this closeness to regional expression makes translation difficult, sometimes impossible when it comes to preserving the flavor of the original. An example of this is the title of Juan Rulfo's story in *El llano en llamas,* "Es que somos muy pobres." A very simple statement to read that becomes impossible to translate because of that *es que.* It precludes a translation as "We're very poor," and "The fact is, we're very poor" would remove it from the mouth of the peasant girl who utters the phrase. There are other cases where customs and manners play a strong role in the formation of words and expressions. Probably the most difficult aspect of translation is the necessary but often futile attempt to preserve or convey a cultural milieu and its concomitants through words. Even within one language different regions produce different nuances and meanings for the same words. A Puerto Rican in Buenos Aires who innocently announces that he is going to catch a bus (*Voy a coger la guagua*) would be arrested as a child molester. *Bicha* in Portugal is a line, a queue; in Brazil it is a drag queen.

When a translator is faced with a work dealing with the pampa and its gauchos, he must be wary of transporting the locale and its inhabitants to the American West. Despite their similarities, the gaucho and the cowboy are two completely different creatures, and Martin Fierro must never sound like Trampas. John Wayne never squatted to sip *mate,* so why should one who does sound like him? I have found that the only solution for such situations, and it is a difficult one to handle, is to invent, in this case, a kind of artificial yet authentic-sounding gaucho or rustic speech in English. As I have said above, when we try to find an existing equivalent we fall ever so short of the mark. I recall asking a Mexican friend about certain purported Mexicanisms in the Spaniard Ramón del Valle-Inclán's novel of Latin American dictatorship and revolution, *Tirano Banderas*. I wondered if he knew if any of these expressions were really Mexican and his reply was no, but they could be. This is what the translator must attempt in cases like these that go across cultures in their idioms.

The Puerto Rican novel *La guaracha del Macho Camacho* (*Macho Camacho's Beat*), by Luis Rafael Sánchez, offered me many difficulties of a cultural nature. It is probably the most "Puerto Rican" novel ever written in that not only the story, but the language itself is so tied to the culture. In the first place, there was the problem of a title. The word *macho*, here an epithet (subsequently picked up by a boxer named Camacho as life continues to imitate art) was no problem as it has become a solid fixture in English and is used by many people who have no Spanish, to the extent that I have even heard *machismo* pronounced with a Germanic *ch*. The guaracha, however, is not as well known as the rhumba or the samba and might even be confused with *cucaracha*, "cockroach," which is a derivation. So, with the author's blessing, I adopted the suggestion put forth by my wife Clementine. Luis Rafael, or Wico, as his friends call him, liked the idea that the word "beat" has a double meaning. It does a fair job of rendering *guaracha* because it has a musical connotation, and it also can imply an itinerary, as in a policeman's beat, and the novel is peripatetic as it traces a route through San Juan and environs. Implicit also could be a Kerouacian sense, but in a broader feeling because we are a generation removed, the aftermath, as it were. This shift in the direction of the title shows once again that translation is an approach and not an equivalency and that a word-for-word technique can often render the translation pallid and ineffective. Faulkner's novel *Light in August* has been given in Spanish as *Luz en agosto*, perfect in a direct matching of words. What Mr. Will had in mind, however, was the country expression used for a cow who is "comin' in," expectant, "heavy in June, light in August." The Spanish is far from that meaning and only preserves the mysterious lyricism of the title.

Sometimes censorship or bowdlerization will affect the translation of a title. A recent example is the novel *South of Nowhere*, by the Portuguese writer António Lobo Antunes. The book deals with Portugal's colonial wars in Africa, which led up to the April revolution and the downfall of the post-Salazarian dictatorship. The English title conveys the idea of a faraway and dismal place, but the Portuguese is ever so much more direct and pithy: *Os Cus de Judas* (Judas's Arses). English has a closely parallel expression, also used quite often in military campaigns, "the asshole of the earth." It would seem, however, that American sensibilities are still too delicate to see any of the "words" on a dust jacket, even though they may be acceptable inside. Not only did the Portuguese strike a blow for political freedom, but they have moved ahead of us in freedom of expression. (At this writing I am faced with a dilemma in the translation of another novel by Antunes. It is a situation akin to the problem offered by the title of *La guaracha del Macho Camacho*. Also using a local type of song, Antunes calls the book *Fado Alexandrino*. As many, but not enough, people know, the *fado* is Portugal's national song, and the alexandrine refers to versification. The problem is still unresolved.)

This matter of choice in translation always leaves the door open to that other possibility. We cannot be sure of ourselves. Translation is a disturbing craft because there is precious little certainty about what we are doing, which makes it so difficult in this age of fervent belief and ideology, this age of greed and screed. To paraphrase Villon in a way that would have suited Montaigne, "Où sont les que sais-je d'antan?" The translator must be alert to that other possibility (or possibilities), even if it doesn't rise up and bite him on the buttocks. He must assume the mind of the old Vermonter, who always sees that other side. When asked by the evangelist, "Friend, have you found Jesus?" his perfectly logical reply is, "God, I didn't know he was lost." The translator can never be sure of himself, he must never be. He must always be dissatisfied with what he does because ideally, platonically, there is a perfect solution, but he will never find it. He can never enter into the author's being and even if he could the difference in languages would preclude any exact reproduction. So he must continue to approach, nearer and nearer, as near as he can, but, like Tantalus, at some practical point he must say ne plus ultra and sink back down as he considers his work done, if not finished (in all senses of the word).

BUILDING A TRANSLATION, THE RECONSTRUCTION BUSINESS: POEM 145 OF SOR JUANA INES DE LA CRUZ

MARGARET SAYERS PEDEN

A more serious title for this essay, which will address aspects of the process of translation, would be "Reading Poem 145 of Sor Juana Inés de la Cruz: Variation on a Sonnet." Metaphorically speaking, however, each of the "variations" can be considered the product of a builder in the reconstruction business.

For Walter Benjamin a translation had to fit itself into its own language "with loving particularity . . . just as the broken pieces of a vase, to be joined again, must fit at every point, though none may be exactly like the other."[1] One can understand why a translator would not be thrilled with this figure—the marks of the patching are all too readily observable, the translator's work distressingly exposed. I like to think of the original work as an ice cube. During the process of translation the cube is melted. While in its liquid state, every molecule changes place; none remains in its original relationship to the others. Then begins the process of forming the work in a second language. Molecules escape, new molecules are poured in to fill the spaces, but the lines of molding and mending are virtually invisible. The work exists in the second language as a new ice cube—different, but to all appearances the same.

The reference in the title, the role of the translator as a builder in the reconstruction business, derives not from reading on translation but from the play "La mueca" by the Argentine psychiatrist-dramatist Eduardo Pavlovsky. One of Pavlovsky's characters, El Sueco, voices his—and perhaps the author's—aesthetic: "Hay que violentar para embellecer; hay que destruir para crear." One must do violence before one can make beauty; one must destroy before one can create. This is scarcely an original idea; rather, a recyclable constant that arises periodically clad in the robes of a new aesthetic.

Margaret Sayers Peden is professor of Spanish in the Department of Romance Languages at the University of Missouri. She has translated works by Isabel Allende, Octavio Paz, Ernesto Sábato, and her translations of Carlos Fuentes include *Terra Nostra, The Hydra Head, Burnt Water, Distant Relations,* and *The Old Gringo.*

1. "The Task of the Translator," translated by James Hynd and M. Valk, *Delos* 2 (1969): 90.

What is striking, however, was how perfectly it described the act of literary translation. We cannot translate until we "do violence" to the original literary work. We must destroy—de-struct (and we must make the obligatory disclaimer: no reference is intended to the terminology of Derrida, who has pre-empted a word I should like to use) before we can re-*con*struct. The translation as edifice seems particularly appropriate for two series of translations with which I have recently been obsessed. The first is Pablo Neruda's *Odas elementales.* In terms of the metaphor, the ode may be seen as one of the log cabins we sometimes find in our architecturally underprivileged land: pared to essentials, elegant in its simplicity, *elemental.* To translate the ode we act as a member of a Preservation Society would act. Carefully, we mark the logs by number, dismantle them, and reconstruct them in new territory, artfully restoring the logs to their original relationships and binding them together with a minimal application of mortar. My quarrel with many early translators of Neruda's odes is that once the cabin of an ode (or a similar poem from one of Neruda's later periods) was constructed, the translator continued to slather on plaster, covering the simplicity of the logs with swirling lines and flourishes that completely obscured the original structure.

The second series of translations that seem particularly receptive to architectural metaphor are the sonnets of Sor Juana Inés de la Cruz. This is undoubtedly because the sonnet is inherently an architectural form. Sor Juana's sonnets are baroque edifices in miniature. To translate them, the artisan must peel away the ornamental gold leaf, remove the convoluted detail of the ornate façade, and strip away baroque accretions until she reaches the structural frame. All the debris—the components of the original edifice—must be transported to a new language, to be restored to its original baroque splendor with the least possible signs of damage.

Two questions arise immediately. Is it possible? And, is it worth the effort? The second question is the easier to answer. Yes! To answer the first would necessitate a lengthy digression, for it touches on the basic question of translatability. The purpose of this exercise is merely to test the efficacy of an architectural model for de-struction and re-construction by applying it to a number of translations of a single sonnet by Sor Juana, poem 145, commonly titled "A su retrato" (To Her Portrait). I wish to reiterate that the sonnet is particularly suited to such analysis and I am aware the term "architecture" would be highly inappropriate when applied to many other types of poems—a poem that depends on musicality, say, or word play, for its being.

"A su retrato" is one of Sor Juana's most widely anthologized poems and pursues themes common to her writing and to the writing of her age: the treachery of illusion and the inevitability of disillusion.

Este, que ves, engaño colorido,
que del arte ostentando los primores,
con falsos silogismos de colores
es cauteloso engaño del sentido:
    éste, en quien la lisonja ha pretendido
excusar de los años los horrores,
y venciendo del tiempo los rigores,
triunfar de la vejez y del olvido,
    es un vano artificio del cuidado,
es una flor al viento delicada,
es un resguardo inútil para el hado:
    es una necia diligencia errada,
es un afán caduco y, bien mirado,
es cadáver, es polvo, es sombra, es nada.

The trot de-structs the sonnet:

This, that you see, colored (false appearance) fraud (hoax,
    deception),
which of art showing (exhibiting, bragging) the beauty
    (exquisiteness),
with false (treacherous, deceitful) syllogisms of colors
is cautious (wary, prudent) fraud (hoax, deception) of the sense
    (reason):
    this, on which flattery (adulation) has attempted (claimed,
    sought)
to excuse (avoid, prevent, exempt) from years the horrors (fright,
    dread),
and conquering (defeating, subduing) from time the rigors (severity,
    cruelty),
triumph from (over) old age (decay) and forgetfulness (oversight,
    oblivion),
    is a vain (empty, futile) artifice (trick, cunning) of care (fear,
    anxiety),
is a flower on the wind (air, gale, breeze) delicate (refined, tender),
is a useless (fruitless, frivolous) guard (defense) for fate (destiny):

is a foolish (stupid, injudicious) diligence (activity, affair) erring
(mistaken),
is a worn out (senile, perishable) anxiety (trouble, eagerness), and,
well considered
is cadaver (dead body), is dust (powder), is shadow (shade, ghost,
spirit), is nothing (nothingness, naught, nonentity; very little)

Here one sees the validity of El Sueco's "hay que violentar";
the trot is an act of pure violence performed on a literary work. It
destroys the integrity of the sonnet, reducing it to an assemblage
of words and lines that may convey minimal meaning, but no artistry. The devastation from this de-struction is so total that, con-
currently, we want to de-struct the sonnet in a different way, within
its own language, reducing it not to word clusters strung along a
narrative line but to its architectural frame: its essential communication. We thus isolate the content that transmits Sor Juana's philosophical views on the fleeting joy of beauty represented in a portrait: the *illusion* that seems to triumph over time by eternalizing
beauty in the oils of the canvas, and the *deceit* inherent in this counterfeit beauty. Beauty, Sor Juana warns, is not eternal. Nor life itself, as we read in the famous, beautiful, and didactic last line of
the sonnet. As beauty yields before time, life itself yields to death:
cadáver evolves into *polvo, polvo* into *sombra, sombra* into *nada.* The
accompanying diagram removes the ornamental—and to a degree
functional—facade to reveal the structural frame.
    The de-structed sonnet reveals the promise—and then the
striking interruption—of parallelism in the two quatrains. Each be-

Este, que ves, engaño colorido,
que del arte ostentando los primores,
con falsos silogismos de colores
es cauteloso engaño del sentido:

éste en quien la lisonja ha pretendido
excusar de los años los horrores,
y venciendo del tiempo los rigores,
triunfar de la vejez y del olvido,

es un vano artificio del cuidado,
es una flor al viento delicada,
es un resguardo inútil para el hado:

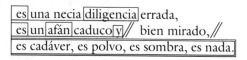

es una necia diligencia errada,
es un afán caduco y// bien mirado,//
es cadáver, es polvo, es sombra, es nada.

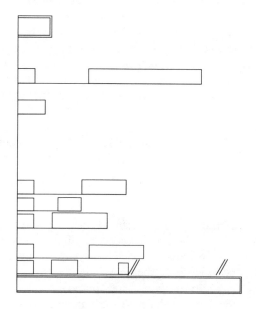

gins with the word *éste*—the pronoun substituting for the word "portrait," which, interestingly, never appears in the sonnet. It is the repetition of *éste* as the first word in line 5 that leads the reader to expect symmetry in the quatrains. (Peripherally, although the first eight lines of an Italianate sonnet are thought of as an octave, the *abba, abba* pattern of the rhyme scheme, as well as the indentation of line 5 in Sor Juana's sonnet, as reproduced in her *Obras completas,* tend to suggest two quatrains.)

The first quatrain is self-contained; every phrase refers to the first word and could be read in this way: "éste, que ves"; "éste, que es engaño colorido"; "éste, del arte ostentando los primores"; "éste, con falsos silogismos de colores"; "éste es engaño del sentido." In contrast to the first, closed quatrain, the second is open: now *éste* promises a closure that is not forthcoming. In lieu of the suggested, but failed, symmetry with "éste . . . es," the second quatrain presents a secondary structural parallelism in the two verb clauses de-

pendent on "en quien la lisonja ha pretendido" and introduced by
excusar and *triunfar* (on which flattery has sought . . . to excuse . . .
and to triumph). Actually, the second quatrain can be read as a long
aside to, or restatement of, the first quatrain. The subject *éste* is
never completed by the verb, which is the *es* of line 9—and all
following lines. The effect of this distancing between subject and
verb is to impel the reader toward the lines of the sestet.

On first view, the six lines of the sestet (conventionally, but not
functionally, broken by a semicolon), appear to be parallel, the *es*
of each line repetitively completing the *éste* of lines 1 and 5. *Éste* is,
equally, *artificio, flor,* and on through *nada.* The parallelism is de-
ceptive, however. There is an important break at the end of the
penultimate line, indicated by "y, bien mirado" (and, well-
considered). The qualities attributed to the portrait before the
break are negative—*artificio, flor delicada* (artifice, delicate
flower)—but not vital. Following the break, we are privy to the
author's deepest beliefs and emotions. It is not merely beauty that
is transitory; life itself resolves into *nada.*

A comparison of the architecture of the translations to the original
reveals to what degree, in the process of reconstruction, they have
been able to duplicate the original frame. The graphs isolate and
replicate, as nearly as possible, the structural components bared in
the graph of Sor Juana's sonnet. It becomes immediately visible
that some damage—from minimal to great—occurs in every moving process.[2]

2. Samuel Beckett, trans., in *An Anthology of Mexican Poetry,* edited by Octavio
Paz and translated by Samuel Beckett (Bloomington: Indiana University Press,
1965), p. 85; John A. Crow, trans., in *An Anthology of Spanish Poetry* (Baton Rouge:
Louisiana State University Press), p. 119; Kate Flores, trans., in *An Anthology of
Spanish Poetry from Garcilaso to García Lorca,* edited by Angel Flores (Garden City:
Anchor Books, 1961), p. 147; Roderick Gill, trans., in Ermilo Abreu Gómez, "The
Poet Nun," reprinted from *Américas,* bimonthly magazine published by the General
Secretariat of the Organization of American States in English and in Spanish, 3
(October 1951): 17; Muna Lee, trans., in *The Epic of Latin American Literature,*
edited by Arturo Torres-Rioseco (New York: Oxford University Press, 1942), p.
38; Frederick Bliss Luquiens, trans., "Spanish American Literature," *Yale Review* 17
(1928): 539; B.G.P., trans., *Translations from Hispanic Poets* (New York: Hispanic
Society of America, 1938), p. 220; Margaret Sayers Peden, trans., *Nimrod* 16
(Spring–Summer, 1983): 82; G. W. Umphrey, trans., *Fantasy* 10 (1942): 43. Unfortunately, Alan Trueblood's *Sor Juana Anthology* (Cambridge: Harvard University
Press, 1988) was published too recently to be used in this essay.

This coloured counterfeit that thou beholdest,
vainglorious with the excellencies of art,
is, in fallacious syllogisms of colour,
nought but a cunning dupery of sense;

this in which flattery has undertaken
to extenuate the hideousness of years,
and, vanquishing the outrages of time,
to triumph o'er oblivion and old age,

is an empty artifice of care,
is a fragile flower in the wind,
is a paltry sanctuary from fate,

is a foolish sorry labour lost,
is conquest doomed to perish and, // well taken, //
is corpse and dust, shadow and nothingness.

                    Samuel Beckett

This artifice of colors that you see
Which boasts the fairest vanities of art,
Ere its false logic and its gloss depart
Will dupe the senses and the memory.

[Here] flattery immune to time's outrage
Has cancelled out the horrors of the years,
And foiling their dread ravages appears
To vanquish both forgetfulness and age.

It is a shallow counterfeit of pride,
A fragile flower that opened in the wind,
A paltry refuge when fate closed the door,

It is a foolish caution put aside,
An outworn zeal that time has bent and thinned;
It is a corpse, dust, shadow, nothing more.

                    John A. Crow

What [here] you see in deceiving tints,
Vaunting its crafty artistry
In specious syllogisms of color,
Is a discreet delusion of the sense;

This which flattery would fain pretend
Could expiate the horrors of the years,
The cruelties of time obliterate,
And triumph over age and nothingness,

'Tis but of apprehensiveness a futile artifice,
'Tis but a brittle blossom in the wind,
'Tis against fate an unavailing wall,

'Tis merely a folly diligently mistaken,
'Tis merely a senile ardor, and // truly seen //
'Tis a corpse, dust, shadow, nothing at all

Kate Flores

This that you see, the false presentment planned
With finest art and all the colored shows
And reasonings of shade, doth but disclose
[is]   The poor deceits by earthly senses fanned!

[Here] where in constant flattery expand
Excuses for the stains that old age knows,
Pretexts against the years' advancing snows,
The foot prints of old seasons to withstand;

'Tis but vain artifice of scheming minds;
'Tis but a flower fading on the winds;
'Tis but a useless protest against Fate;

'Tis but stupidity without a thought,
A lifeless shadow, // if we meditate; //
'Tis death, 'tis dust, 'tis shadow, yea, 'tis nought.

Roderick Gill

This that you gaze upon, a painted lie,
Blazoning forth the niceties of art
With false syllogisms the hues impart,
Is a shrewd snare, the sense being ta'en thereby.

This, wherein the flatteries try to cover
The horrors of the years, and to erase
The rigors Time has stamped upon the face,
Age and forgetfulness to triumph over:

Is an artifice most vainly wrought,
Is a frail flower carried on the wind,
Is a shield against a sure Fate borne,

Is the idle labor of a vagrant mind,
Is a solicitude ponderous and out-worn,
Is corpse—is dust—is shadow—and is nought!

Muna Lee

This that you see before you testifies
To the great skill and craft of one well-taught
In art. Its clever syllogisms wrought
Of multicolored paint,[   ] deceive your eyes;

[Its] deft and cunning loveliness defies
The years to come, with toil and trouble fraught,
Challenging all that time shall bring to naught,
And all that withers when the flower dies.

What of it? Fate will not for long restrain
Her hand. The flower, after all, will fade, in stress
Of winter wind, nor ever grow again.

And then, I think, the artist will confess
That this his handiwork is all in vain;
Is dead, is dust, is painted nothingness.

Frederick Bliss Luquiens

This trickery of paint which you perceive
With all the finest hues of art enwrought,
Which is false argument of colours taught
By subtle means the [   ] senses to deceive—

This by which foolish woman would believe
She could undo the evil years have brought
And conquering in the war against time fought
Could triumph over age, and youth retrieve—

Is all a futile ruse that she has tried,
A fragile flower tossed against the wind,
A useless bribe the power of fate to appease,

A silly effort of mistaken pride,
A base desire, and // viewed in rightful mind,//
Is dust, a corpse, a shade—is less than these.

B.G.P.

This that you gaze on, colorful deceit,
that so immodestly displays art's favors,
with its fallacious arguments of colors
is to the senses cunning counterfeit,

this on which kindness practiced to delete
from cruel years accumulated horrors,
constraining time to mitigate its rigors,
and thus oblivion and age defeat,

is but artifice a sop to vanity,
is but a flower by the breezes bowed,
is but a ploy to counter destiny,

is but a foolish labor ill-employed,
is but a fancy, and, // as all may see,//
is but cadaver, ashes, shadow, void.

Margaret Sayers Peden

This [portrait] so attractive to the eyes,
[This painting] that beguiles with cunning art,
A synthesis of colors that impart
A false impression of the things we prize;

This [painted thing] in which the artist's skill
Has tried to check the ravages of age,
The rigors of the passing years assuage,
And save me from oblivion's ruthless will:

But all in vain! 'Tis a fragile flower,
'Tis but a feeble artifice of thought,
A frail defence indeed against the power

Of fate, a trifle diligently wrought,
The worthless effort of a passing hour,
Inanimated dust, a thing of naught.

G. W. Umphrey

These comparisons are not meant to suggest that a translation can, or even should, slavishly follow in a second language the syntactical arrangement of the first. What these graphs do illustrate is the importance to the re-constructed edifice of a sound structure. When the frame disappears, the edifice collapses of its own weight.

Even when a translator has mounted a viable frame, the process of reconstruction has only begun. The outlines of the edifice must be fleshed out and the distinguishing marks of its original beauty restored. Now the translator must sift through the rubble of his or her de-struction and rescue such materials as meter, rhyme, vocabulary, rhetorical tone, poetic figure, and period.

We might begin with period, as it subsumes other elements such as vocabulary and rhetorical tone. Certainly the problems of period are pertinent to the sonnet. Today relatively few people read, very few poets write, sonnets. At the same time, the sonnet has survived in almost inviolable form. We may conceive of a sonnet without rhyme, but we cannot call a poem a sonnet in English unless it is written in fourteen lines of iambic pentameter. The translator of sonnet 145, then, is faced with a form encrusted with centuries of tradition, one whose formalism dictates a sympathetic formality in lexicon and tone. Each of the translations reflects this deference to the sonnet in general and to Sor Juana's century in particular. In elevating the language of the poem, each translator knowingly proceeds against the grain of contemporary poetry. Each of the nine translators has paid homage to a more formal period in the choice of vocabulary. The translations are sprinkled with words like "dupery," "vainglorious," "expiate," "specious syllogisms," "fallacious," and "mitigate," as well as consciously antiquated phrases such as "Thou beholdest," "sorry labour lost," "doth but disclose" and "on which kindness practiced to delete." No translator constructed Sor Juana's sonnet using modern vocabulary or contemporary rhetoric. Seven of the nine translators felt sufficiently constrained by the tradition of form to elect rhyme and meter in their reconstructions. Though rhyme and meter are not content, they are components that cannot be artificially separated *from* content, any more than plaster takes form without a substructure of lathe or pebble. Conversely, when the frame of the translation is slapdash, it is usually the result of subordination of structure to the ornamentation of meter or rhyme. When end-words like "pride," "bent and thinned," "wall," "snows," "mind," "door," "skill," and "power" intrude into the translations, we know they have no counterpart in the Spanish but are aberrations caused by the exigencies of meter and rhyme.

The rhyme scheme of the Petrarchan or Italianate sonnet (typically *abba, abba, cdcdcd* in Sor Juana's sonnets) demands almost impossible acrobatics from the English-language translator. We are aware of the reasons. It is not crucial that two translators rejected rhyme. What is more serious, however, is the philosophical decision to ignore, or slight, meter, to align a poem in an external frame that suggests a sonnet but does not replicate the rhythm of a sonnet's lines. Beckett's translation, with some effort, can be scanned as a five-beat, nonmetrical line. The Flores cannot be scanned metrically.

Like the difficulties of rhyme, those of meter are contained within linguistic peculiarities. The English and Spanish lines are built from different rhythms. The Spanish speaker counts syllables; the English speaker counts stresses, or beats. Syllabic count does exist in English but is uncommon. One might think that the Spanish hendecasyllabic line (count of 11) would correspond without great difficulty of adaptation with the five feet (count of 10) of iambic pentameter. This is not the case. For reasons that are unclear to me, an hendecasyllabic line translated into English almost inevitably adjusts to four feet. Thus it becomes necessary for the translator to "pad" the lines, to add intrusive foreign materials, in order to make the Spanish edifice conform to English style. No further comment is necessary on the numerous pitfalls that await the unwary translator in this endeavor.

Poetic figures in sonnet 145 are most notable in the sestet and take the form of metaphor, not simile: *éste* (the portrait) is "artificio del cuidado," "flor al viento" and, of course, "cadáver, polvo, sombra, nada." When the metaphor is material, that is, an object like a flower, or even a cadaver, the original figure is successfully paralleled in the translations: "a fragile flower," "a brittle blossom," "a cadaver," or "a corpse." When the metaphor is an abstraction we find the translations much less precise. For example, "Un resguardo inútil" becomes variously, and variantly, "a shield against a sure Fate," "a useless bribe," "a ploy to counter destiny," "a frail defence," "a paltry sanctuary," "a paltry refuge," "against fate an unavailing wall," and in Lee's translation, something completely indecipherable.

The questions proliferate. How do these translations conform to the traditional classifications of translation: literal, approximation, or adaptation/imitation? How much is lost if the English-language reader does not hear—cannot, of course, hear—the allusions to Góngora in the sonnet's last line? Did faint echoes of Villon's "où sont les neiges d'antan" somehow suggest Gill's "the years' advancing snows"? What would a concordance of cognates reveal? Why does only one translator make use of the crutch of the cognate slant rhyme of favors/colors/horrors/rigors (for *primores/colores/horrores/rigores*)? What is the effect of alliteration in the English (as in "brittle blossom," "discreet delusion")? Why do the reconstructions of the secondary parallelism in the second quatrain range from perfect recreation to total disregard? Most important of all, how is the key line of sonnet 145 translated? This last question is one we cannot ignore.

In my first comments on the poem's structure I pointed out how everything impels the reader toward that last line. As it is the essential line, it is the line the translator must translate with greatest care. Perversely, it is the most difficult, technically. Among the reasons are the fact that the words are stated so as to allow no interpretation, and when inflexibility of meaning is added to the demands of meter and rhyme the difficulty is raised to the tenth power. In addition, there are the problems of the word *nada* itself; it is one of the beautiful words in the Spanish language, and one of the most difficult to translate. The trot offers "nothing," "nothingness," "naught," "nonentity," and "very little"—none of which is strikingly mellifluous. Neither, with the possible exception of "naught," does any lend itself easily to rhyme. Beckett, unperturbed by problems of rhyme, chose "nothingness," a not unpleasant word if one can forgive it the awkwardness of being naturally dactyllic in a line that demands an iamb. Crow rhymes "nothing more" with door, which might be cited as a prime example of necessity being the "portal" to invention. Flores, like Beckett indifferent to rhyme, ends with "nothing at all." Gill and Lee find rhyme for "nought" in "thought" (Gill) and "wrought" (Lee), Gill waxing more elaborate, "'tis . . . 'tis . . . 'tis . . . yea, 'tis nought," and Lee, more simply, "Is . . . is . . . is . . . and is nought!" Luquiens forces the meter of nothingness for rhyme with "stress" and "confess." B.G.P.'s solution is "less than these," rhyming with "appease." My translation deserts the "nothing" words for an equally difficult-to-rhyme "void," resorting to the near, or slant, rhyme of "bowed" and the true rhyme of "ill-employed." And Umphrey makes "naught" the choice of the majority, rhyming both with "thought" and "wrought."

What may we have learned from this exercise? Facetiously, that the moving and re-construction trade is not without its perils. More seriously, to the serious critic of translation—not the reviewer who crawls through a translation on his hands and knees, dictionary in hand, nosing out words for which he does not find a hundred percent correspondence from language to language—I have offered a formula. Thus the reader-critic may approach the reading of a sonnet translation—and perhaps that of other formal poetry as well—by measuring basic structure as well as evaluating ornamentation. I remind the translator always to be alert to the *total* structure of the sonnet. This is particlarly pertinent in sonnet 145, which consists of a single sentence. It is easy to think of this poem in terms of units contained within the rhyme scheme (two quatrains of *abba* rhyme, plus a sestet) or as units determined by typography. As she conserves the integrity of the design, the translator must also monitor how rhyme and meter distort and stress the structure, how words, rhetorical figures, even concepts, can be twisted out of shape by the very effort to adorn the edifice with beauty and symmetry.

Reading nine translations of sonnet 145, we have seen the poem de-structed, and observed the failures and successes of its reconstruction. Those failures and successes reveal to us the strengths and weaknesses of the original poem as well.

We have isolated the techniques by which Sor Juana impels the poem toward the last line; seen—though not every translator judged it important—the imperious repetition that both postpones and presses toward the didactic last line. What we might not have seen, were it not for the magnifying lens the translations focus upon the poem, are lines where the poem itself is "soft." We have noted that the metaphors of the sestet are laxly translated. With the exception of the material figure of the flower, and the crutch offered by the cognate "artifice," the translations of lines 9 through 13 bear virtually no resemblance to each other. To a degree the discrepancies can be ascribed to the translators, but they are not totally at fault. The imprecision lies in the original lines. Sor Juana, too, was directed by rhyme: note, for example, the displacement of the adjective *delicada,* the near redundancy of *necia* and *errada.* Sor Juana's eye is fixed on *nada.* She is marking time in the five lines preceding the final line, letting rhyme and rhythm and repetition bear her toward the culmination of the poem. The seemingly sound architecture of the sestet is actually trompe l'oeil. The sonnet, reduced to its fundament, is contained in the first word and the last line: "Éste . . . es cadáver, es polvo, es sombra, es nada." Any further reduction would lead to a blank page.

All translations should be followed by a blank page. That blank page awaits the ideal translation of poem 145, the reconstituted vase, the re-formed ice cube, the perfectly re-constructed baroque edifice.

TRANSLATING MEDIEVAL
EUROPEAN POETRY
BURTON RAFFEL

One can, and comparists do, generalize about medieval European
literature as a whole. The translator of a medieval work, however,
is far more limited, for by the very nature of his task he must enter
as deeply and totally as he is able into a specific text, produced in a
specific language, at a specific (or approximately specific) time, and
in a specific tradition. Each of these components presents him with
a problem in re-creation as well as in translation: medieval texts
result from authorial intentions very different from those of our
own time; medieval languages have very different linguistic features from modern ones; the context of life has changed enor-
mously from those times to this one; and medieval literary traditions are today either dead, or poorly understood, or both. The
translator of medieval poetry must try to think, and then to write,
like the poet he is translating, and not like any other poet. This,
too, is typical of translation as a whole, for the translation process
is never a generalizing one. It is always relentlessly specific: the
original text neither can nor should be evaded. But translating
medieval European poetry is an even more time- and place-bound
process than translating more recent work.

European literature has four main chronological divisions:
classical, medieval, renaissance, and modern. Precise dates are not
necessary: the chronology is hardly a fixed and immutable one. But
quite apart from matters of chronology, translating poetry means
recreating in one language the feelings and forms of expression of
another language. Yet language aside, which of these two poetic
samples seems older, seems more distant from the forms and
expressions of our own contemporary world?[1]

Odi et amo: quare id faciam, fortase requiris.
nescio, sed fieri sentio et excrucior.

Burton Raffel is distinguished professor of humanities at the University of South-
western Louisiana. Of particular interest to the field of translation studies are his
books *The Forked Tongue: A Study of the Translation Process* (1971) and *The Art of
Translating Poetry* (1988). He has edited *An Anthology of Modern Indonesian Poetry*
(1964) and *From the Vietnamese: Ten Centuries of Poetry* (1968).

1. Catullus, *The Complete Poetry*, translated by Frank O. Copley (Ann Arbor:
University of Michigan Press, 1957), p. 104; *Beowulf*, translated by Burton Raffel
(New York: Mentor/New American Library, 1963), p. 23.

I hate and I love
well, why do I, you probably ask
I don't know, but I know it's happening
and it hurts

F. O. Copley

Hwaet, we Gardena in geardagum,
theodcyniga thrym gefrunon,
hu tha aethelingas ellen fremedon! [spelling normalized]

Hear me! We've heard of Danish heroes,
Ancient kings and the glory they cut
For themselves, swinging mighty swords!

B. Raffel

The first sample is a brief but complete Latin poem by Catullus. The second is the famous opening of the Old English *Beowulf.* Roughly a thousand years separates the two examples. But can anyone doubt that Catullus is in virtually every way more "modern"— in subject, poetic approach, use of language, sophistication of feeling, nature of feeling, and so on?

Having myself translated from three bodies of medieval poetry, Old English (roughly 700–1100), Middle English (roughly 1000–1500), and Old French (roughly 900–1450), I propose to stick closely to these three reasonably well demarcated areas, and in particular to the three long poems I have translated, the Old English *Beowulf,* the Middle English *Sir Gawain and the Green Knight,* and the Old French of Chrétien de Troyes' *Yvain.* I have recently published *The Art of Translating Poetry,* in which I try to deal with at least some of the more generalized aesthetic, cultural, and linguistic issues I must here more or less resolutely ignore. But if I am to say anything remotely sensible about translating medieval European poetry, I am obliged to work with specific texts and their specific contexts.

I have cited the opening of *Beowulf.* It will be easier to get at what is distinctly medieval about that poem if we look at the beginning of a classical epic, once again almost a millennium older. Here are the first lines of Virgil's *Aeneid:*[2]

---

2. Virgil, *The Aeneid,* translated by Robert Fitzgerald (New York: Random House, 1983), p. 3.

Arma virumque cano, Troiae qui primus ab oris
Italiam fato profugus Lavinaque venit
litora, multum ille et terris iactatus et alto
vi superum, saevae memorem Iunonis ob iram,
multa quoque et bello passus, dum conderet urbem
inferretque deos Latio, genus under Latinum
Albanique patres atque altae moenia Romae.

I sing of warfare and a man at war.
From the sea-coast of Troy in earlier days
He came to Italy by destiny,
To our Lavinian western shore,
A fugitive, this captain, buffeted
Cruelly on land as on the sea
By blows from powers of the air—behind them
Baleful Juno in her sleepless rage.
And cruel losses were his lot in war,
Till he could found a city and bring home
His gods to Latium, land of the Latin race,
The Alban lords, and the high walls of Rome.

                                        Robert Fitzgerald

One usually speaks of Latin's intense concentration. It is there, of
course. Manifestly, the translator has had to use twelve lines where
the Latin has only seven. No translator can possibly reproduce Latin's concentration in English; Fitzgerald seems to me to have done
the job as well as it can be done. And he has equally well rendered
Virgil's poetry, its tone, its movement. His English version shows
clearly that the Latin poet is deeply self-conscious—self-conscious
about his own role, self-conscious about his country's history, destiny, and significance, and self-conscious about the likely place his
poem will fill. "Tantaene animis caelestibus irae?" Virgil asks, a few
lines further. "Are there such immense resentments in heavenly
minds?" The question is, like so much in the *Aeneid*, strictly rhetorical. Of course such resentments flourish in heavenly as they do
in earthbound minds. Virgil knows that perfectly well, and so does
his audience. But for the purposes of his poem Virgil assumes a
reflective stance which is in truth not so much reflective as it is,
once more, self-conscious. Aeneas is the founder of Rome. He
must therefore emerge not only as obedient to the gods, but in a
sense as superior to them—just as, in Virgil's mind, and also in his
audience's mind, Rome is plainly superior to anything and everything that either has been or ever will be on the face of the earth.

Horace did not share this confidence; neither did Catullus. But then, they did not write epics, and Virgil did.

Thus the poem's self-consciousness, which is what I want to emphasize and the reason I have brought the *Aeneid* into this discussion, is neither a defect nor an accident. It is an integral part of what the *Aeneid* is all about. No matter that Virgil, too, surely had doubts about "the glory that was Greece, And the grandeur that was Rome." What is infinitely more significant is that he spent long years laboring at the *Aeneid*, and felt it so unfinished that, at his death, he tried to have the manuscript destroyed. The poem's self-conscious proclamations could not have been more deliberate choices, nor could those choices have seemed more important to the poet.

The *scop* ("showp," bard, poet) who gave us *Beowulf* starts from a far more defensive posture.

> Beowulf waes breme—blaed wide sprang—
> Scyldes eafera Scedelandum in.
> Swa sceal geong guma gode gewyrcean,
> fromum feohgiftum on faeder bearme,
> thaet hine on ylde eft gewunigen
> wilgesithas, thonne wig cume,
> leode gelaesten; lofdaedum sceal
> in maegtha gehwaere man getheon.

> Beo('s) . . . power and fame soon spread through the world.
> Shild's strong son was the glory of Denmark;
> His father's warriors were wound round his heart
> With golden rings, bound to their prince
> By his father's treasure. So young men build
> The future, wisely open-handed in peace,
> Protected in war; so warriors earn
> Their fame, and wealth is shaped with a sword.
>
> B. Raffel

The *Beowulf scop* lived in a different age. His poem aims to defend hard-won devices created in order to hold together a constantly splintering, often brutally militaristic society. The *Aeneid*'s audience needed to know how high above ordinary societies Rome soared. *Beowulf*'s audience, and particularly the princes and kings to whom it was in my judgment specifically directed, needed to know how to keep their world from collapsing. The last lines of the *Aeneid,* and especially Aeneas's furious declaration of revenge, are a burst of confident power:

> "tune hinc spoliis indute meorum
> eripiare mihi? Pallas te hoc vulnere, Pallas
> immolat et poenam scelerato ex sanguine sumit."
> hoc dicens ferrum adverso sub pectore condit
> fervidus. ast illi solvuntur frigore membra,
> vitaque cum gemitu fugit indignata sub umbras.

> "You in your plunder, torn from one of mine,
> Shall I be robbed of you? This wound will come
> From Pallas: Pallas makes this offering
> And from your criminal blood exacts his due."

> He sank his blade in fury in Turnus' chest.
> Then all the body slacked in death's chill,
> And with a groan for that indignity
> His spirit fled into the gloom below.
>
> Robert Fitzgerald

But as Beowulf prepares to die, mortally wounded in a fight with a dragon, he gasps—and I give the next passage only in translation (my own), for the point I wish to make is aimed entirely at the translation:

> "For this, this gold, these jewels, I thank
> Our Father in Heaven, Ruler of the Earth—
> For all of this, that His grace has given me,
> Allowed me to bring to my people while breath
> Still came to my lips. I sold my life
> For this treasure, and I sold it well. Take
> What I leave, Wiglaf, lead my people,
> Help them; my time is gone."

What Wiglaf in fact says is a long, bitter denunciation of those who ran when Beowulf most needed them, ending with the curse that "Death / Would be better . . . for you than the kind / Of life you can lead, branded with disgrace!" And Wiglaf's point is driven home, lengthily and somberly, by his messenger, sent to inform those not present of Beowulf's death. The messenger speaks for well over a hundred lines, ending:

"These are the quarrels, the hatreds, the feuds,
That will bring us battles, force us into war
With the Swedes, as soon as they've learned how our lord
Is dead, know that the Geats are leaderless,
Have lost the best of kings, Beowulf—
He who held our enemies away,
Kept land and treasure intact, who saved
Hrothgar and the Danes—he who lived
All his long life bravely. . . . Spears shall be lifted,
Many cold mornings, lifted and thrown,
And warriors shall waken to no harp's bright call
But the croak of the dark-black raven, ready
To welcome the dead, anxious to tell
The eagle how he stuffed his craw with corpses,
Filled his belly even faster than the wolves."

And this poem ends, unlike the *Aeneid,* in exactly the same key:

And so Beowulf's followers
Rode, mourning their beloved leader,
Crying that no better king had ever
Lived, no prince so mild, no man
So open to his people, so deserving of praise.

What the translator of *Beowulf* must do, it seems to me, is recognize and, as closely as he is able, transmit the poem's overwhelmingly protective, defensive, almost desperately guardianlike tone. The deliberate, exultant cadences of Virgil must give way to a poetic movement more halting, heavier, more circumscribed. That is in truth the cadence of the Old English: here are the final five lines, already cited in translation:

Swa begnornodon Geata leode
hlafordes hryre, heorthgeneatas;
cwaedon that he waere wyruldcyninga
manna mildust ond monthwaerust,
leodum lithost ond lofgeornost.

We virtually hear, in these lines, a solemn drum intoning the funereal steps, the mournful words, of Beowulf's followers. Most of the poem moves at a similar pace—not ponderous so much as heavy-treading. Even when the oratory mounts, even when there

is a degree of exultation in what is being said, the verse cadence,
and the rhetoric which frames it, keep to a steady, deliberate beat.
Here is Beowulf reporting to his own king on his potent successes
in the difficult art of monster slaying:

"The whole tale of how I killed him,
Repaid him in kind for all the evil
He'd done, would take too long: your people,
My prince, were honored in the doing."

I give my translation first, because I want to emphasize how totally
determined it is by the nature of the Old English original. I think
the same stately, formal, but half-ponderous insistence can be heard
in both:

To lang ys to reccene, hu ic tham leodsceathan
yfla gewhylces ondlean forgeald;
thaer ic, theoden min, thine leode
weorthode weorcum.

If then the lesson is that the translator must listen to his original, must sympathize with (and of course must also understand)
what his original is trying to convey, it is equally important that
the translation be a medium of literary transmission, not merely an
empty echo trying to reproduce, more or less mechanically, the
original's beat. The translator of medieval poetry cannot possibly
reproduce the exact sounds, the exact linguistic effects, of a linguistically long-dead original, any more than he can hope to find exact
verbal equivalences for long-dead turns of phrase. At the start of
Beowulf, for example, we are told that the hero being described
"Oft . . . sceathena threatum, / monegum maegthum medosetla of-
teah." More or less literally (which is manifestly no way ever to
translate anything): "Often . . . (he) took away (deprived) of their
mead-hall seats crowds of enemies, many tribes (peoples, nations)."
Translating this brief passage into prose, rather than verse (another
road that should never be taken by the literary translator), William
Alfred comes up with "More than once, (he) pulled seats in the
mead-hall out from beneath troops of his foes, tribe after tribe."
But is the hero no more than an aberrant practical joker? The cadence has necessarily vanished, when the translator employs prose.
But far more than cadence has vanished, here. I translate the passage: "[He] made slaves of soldiers from every / Land, crowds of

captives he'd beaten / Into terror." Is this what the Old English
says? The answer, simply, is yes, it's exactly what it says—to the
Old English audience for whom it was intended. To deprive a free
warrior of his rightful seat in the mead-hall meant, for them, to
also deprive him of his freedom—that is, to turn him into a slave.
And how, in the Old English world, was this accomplished? In war:
men who were beaten and taken prisoner became slaves, denied
free access to any mead-hall, either their own or their captors'.

What the translator of medieval poetry must do—deeply
understanding and deeply sympathizing with his original—is convey to *his* audience not the bare words of his original text but the
meaning of those words. He must cast his own words in a tone,
and give them a verse movement, as close to that of the original as
he can devise. The translator of modern poetry does this too: of
course. But the task is obviously in many ways a great deal simpler,
in dealing with modern poetry, for the translator of medieval verse
is never translating only words, or even translating only emotions.
The translator of medieval verse is transmitting an entire culture, a
dead worldview, with all its dead customs and turns of phrase—
cast in molds of dead verse form and verse movement. Just as writing is an act of hubris, so too is good translation. The translator
cannot afford to be any more modest than the original author
was—though he must necessarily be a great deal more careful. Indeed, it has been my experience that translators with an excess of
modesty are usually, perhaps even always, translators of poor quality. The scholar is much more appropriately modest. The translator
is, to some extent like the original author, a risk-taker—and risk-
takers must not be modest, or the risks they take are not worth
troubling with.

Beowulf dates from approximately A.D. 800. We know neither the
exact date nor anything whatever about the author. If we come
forward almost seven hundred years, to *Sir Gawain and the Green
Knight,* we find ourselves knowing exactly as much about the
poem's date and its authorship—i.e., nothing. We know a great
deal more about the poem's context, of course. The fact that *Gawain* is at least seven hundred years closer to the modern world
ensures that we have vastly more contemporaneous evidence of all
sorts, to help us in dealing with at least some of the text's uncertainties.

Anything we know, or think we know, about the medieval nature of *Beowulf* needs to be sharply modified, in dealing with *Ga-*

wain. For that same seven-hundred-year span also ensures that *Gawain* is necessarily a very different poem. We inevitably find
ourselves dealing with sharply changed language, with sharply al-
tered verse forms, and reflections of a society which has been many
times transformed—not simply by the passage of hundreds of years
but also by the vast upheavals consequent on the Norman Conquest. In the chronology of English literature, both *Beowulf* and
Gawain are medieval poems. But they come to us out of extraor-
dinarily different literary, linguistic, and social worlds. And their
translators need, as intelligently as they can, to confront those differences directly.

Specifically linguistic pressures, oddly enough, are much less
burdensome than they might at first seem. *Gawain* is an unusual
Middle English text (in this as in other respects). Geoffrey Chaucer's Middle English dialect was the direct antecedent of today's
English. Chaucer can therefore be fairly readily understood by anyone familiar with Modern English; some adjustments, and some
specific vocabulary, are virtually all that is needed. But *Gawain* is
written in an obscure north-country dialect—so obscure, indeed,
that we do not know its exact nature or location. The manuscript
is plainly a scriptorium copy—that is, a commercially produced
version—rather than the author's original. And it is equally plainly
the work of a second-rate, provincial scriptorium: even the illustrations are bad, both as art and as illustrations of this particular text.
The art work in the manuscript does not, for example, show the
green knight as green, nor are his hair and beard notably long,
though the text insists that they are. The obscurity of the poem's
origin makes for some difficult linguistic moments. About as many
words occur uniquely in *Gawain* as occur in *Beowulf,* and uniquely
used words are naturally very hard to pin down. But that same
difficulty also tends to relieve us of the "false friend" problem that
"translators" of Chaucer are obliged to deal with. If Chaucer writes
"A good felawe to have his concubyn," the translator must be careful to turn Middle English "felawe" into Modern English "rascal."
If Chaucer writes, "He was a gentil harlot and a kynde," the translator must turn "gentil" into "worthy" and "harlot" into (once
more) "rascal." And in the process the translator of Chaucer has
lost, in my view, too much, as well as too much that need not be
lost, given the essential similarity rather than difference between
the two forms of English. It is better (and not really very difficult)
for the modern reader to learn a bit of Chaucer's Middle English
vocabulary and read the poet in the original.

But the language of *Gawain* is consistently far more foreign to us than the language of Chaucer. Oddly, as I say, this makes translation simpler (if not easier), because the translator rarely has to worry about words which, over time, have subtly changed their meaning, or about idioms which have changed meaning, or about the whole problem of words which look like modern English but are in fact not at all modern.

Yet the basic syntax of *Gawain*, its grammatical structure and ordering, is very like that of Chaucer, which once again makes the linguistic difficulties still less burdensome. Here are the opening lines, orthographically normalized:

Sithen the sege and the assaut watz sesed at Troye,
The borgh brittened and brent to brondez and askez,
The tulk that the trammes of tresoun ther wroght
Watz tried for his tricherie, the trewest on erthe:
Hit watz Ennias the athel, and his highe kynde,
That sithen depreced prouinces, and patrounes bicome
Welneghe of al the wele in the west iles.

This is marvellously strange stuff, woven on a fabric of relatively standard Middle English syntax, but using a high percentage of regional dialect and Scandinavian borrowings and also employing a late, divergent form of the alliteratively structured verse that we find in *Beowulf*. But *Gawain* is stranger still, for each verse strophe (and no one has yet figured out what if anything determines the length of each such strophe, which varies according to no known pattern) ends with what is called a "bob"—that is, a rhyme word which leads us into a concluding "wheel" of four iambic trimeter lines, the second and fourth of which rhyme with the "bob" word, the first and third of which rhyme with each other. In the first strophe—and I use "strophe" in order to avoid such inapplicable words as "stanza": we haven't any idea what the author of *Gawain* or those with whom he associated called this verse form—the "bob and wheel" looks like this. I set out the bob and wheel in italic, in order to be absolutely clear, though no italic separation occurs in the poem:

On mony bonkkes ful brode Bretayn he settez
    with wynne,
    Where werre and wrake and wonder
    Bi sythez hatz wont therinne,

> *And oft bothe blysse and blunder*
> *Ful skete hatz skyfted synne.*

Were there any doubt about the unusual nature of *Gawain,* surely
this strange combination of formal features would put it to rest.
Although the poem was written about 1390, most of it is composed according to a thinned-out but recognizable version of Old
English prosody—dead, so far as written records tell us, for something over three centuries. Plainly, the so-called alliterative revival
in Middle English, of which *Gawain* is a part, is better called an
alliterative *sur*vival. We have no information on what part of that
survival was oral, or what part was written. And translating oral
literature presents very special problems.[3] But survive the alliterative verse form did, and produced not only this splendid poem but
also a masterpiece like *Piers Plowman. Piers Plowman,* however,
makes no meter-and-rhyme concession to the new and dominant
verse forms so brilliantly employed by Chaucer, verse forms which
were already well on their way to literary dominance in England.
Gawain does make such a concession, in its consistent use of the
bob and wheel—and thereby indicates that its author's cultural
stance was at the same time both regressive and progressive.

But there is much more to that author's peculiar stance, to the
extent we are able to make ourselves understand it. *Beowulf* surely
owes a huge debt to Old Germanic traditions, both in form and in
content. It may owe something to the *Aeneid:* I prefer to leave that
case as speculative, though some fine argument has been made.
Beowulf's Old Testament influences are clear, though not perhaps
overwhelmingly large. *Gawain* owes much to poems like *Beowulf*
(there may well have been other Old English epics, now lost to us;
we do not know, nor do we know if the author of *Gawain* knew of
Beowulf). But *Gawain* also owes a huge debt to the literature of
medieval France, whose stamp is all over the poem. The marks
of current Christian thinking and emotion are large, too—and if
the author of *Gawain* was also the author of other works bound in
the same codex, like *Pearl* (this case, too, is unproven and probably
unprovable), his religious awareness, and training, were extensive.
A poet whose background includes Old English (oral? written?
both?), newfangled moderns like Chaucer, deep currents of
fourteenth-century mystical Christianity, and a wide reading in and

---

3. See "The Manner of Boyan: Translating Oral Literature," *Oral Tradition* 1
(January 1986): 11–29.

appreciation of medieval French masters is surely an odd author if ever there was one. He is a veritable pin cushion of conflicting cultures, simultaneously looking to almost all points of the compass. Representing this swirling literary sea in a modern English translation, accordingly, is fearsomely difficult—and, in fact, the first draft of *Beowulf* (a poem of 3,182 lines) took me six months of concentrated work, but the first draft of *Gawain* (a poem of only 2,530 lines) took me eighteen months.

Let us return to the poem's first seven lines, already reproduced in the original Middle English and clearly not easy to understand (though the poem seems somewhat less craggy in my orthographic normalization). I decided to translate *Gawain* after a group of well-trained graduate students who had a year-long course with me in thirteenth- and fourteenth-century English literature were, in the second half of that year, totally buffaloed by the poem's difficulties. I render the first seven lines like this:[4]

> Once the siege and assault had done for Troy,
> And the city was smashed, burned to ashes,
> The traitor whose tricks had taken Troy
> For the Greeks, Aeneas the noble, was exiled
> For Achilles' death, for concealing his killer,
> And he and his tribe made themselves lords
> Of the western islands, rulers of provinces . . .

Guido de Columnis's *Historia Destructionis Troiae* probably lies behind this version of Aeneas's history (though it is not entirely certain that Aeneas is the traitor being referred to), but that is essentially trivial and certainly not of large importance either to the poet or to us. More significant matters include (*a*) the degree to which the poet's rather rough-and-ready alliteration is reproduced; (*b*) the adaptation in modern English of the French-influenced aspects of the poet's high style; (*c*) the working out of an equivalent to the poem's verse movement, and also of an equivalent to the poem's carefully, even elaborately wrought verse texture; and (*d*) the handling of the meter-and-rhyme bob and wheel. Let me take these seriatim.

Old English alliteration adheres to tight, regular patterns. The great majority of surviving Old English poetry features a line of

---

4. *Sir Gawain and the Green Knight,* translated by Burton Raffel (New York: Mentor/New American Library, 1970), p. 49.

four beats, sometimes with three, sometimes with two, but never with four beats alliterating. The last beat, in particular, never alliterates—as if to quickly, briefly shift gears and give the reader-audience's ear a moment of relief, of change. Nor do either alliterative patterns or the sounds which are alliterated reproduce themselves from line to line: the *scop* had a profound understanding of the need for variety. The basic division of the individual line, something (but not exactly) like a caesura, occurs at the mid point, that is, after the second beat. Enjambment is quite common. (A small percentage of lines features six rather than four beats, though under exactly what circumstances we do not know. The line division then occurs after the third rather than the second beat. The alliterative patterns are slightly different, in this hyper-metrical line, though again we are not sure just what rules are being applied.)[5]

Gawain's alliteration is much more irregular. In these first seven lines, for example, we have the following patterns:

> line 1: 5 beats, the first 4 alliterating
> line 2: ditto
> line 3: 4 beats, the first 3 alliterating
> line 4: ditto
> line 5: 4 beats, the first 2 alliterating
> line 6: 5 beats, the 2d, 3d, and 4th alliterating
> line 7: 4(?) beats, the first 3 alliterating

Any self-respecting Old English *scop* would tear out his hair, seeing workmanship of so fuzzy and unpredictable a kind. But alliteration is of high importance to the *Gawain* poet, whether or not he uses it exactly as his poetic ancestors did, and it must therefore be featured in the translation. In my rendering, we have the following patterns for these same opening lines:

> line 1: 4 beats, the first two alliterating
> line 2: ditto (with, however, an added rhyme as between beats 2 and 4)
> line 3: 4 beats, all alliterating
> line 4: 4 beats, the 2d and 4th alliterating
> line 5: 4 beats, all but the 2d alliterating

5. See Burton Raffel, "*Judith:* Hypermetricity and Rhetoric," in *Anglo-Saxon Poetry*, ed. Lewis E. Nicholson and Dolores Warwick Frese (Notre Dame: University of Notre Dame Press, 1975), pp. 124–34.

line 6: 4 beats, no alliteration
line 7: ditto

In short, what I have done is reproduce much though not all of the poem's alliteration, with occasional gaps for the relief of the modern reader (who needs a good deal more relief than did the original audience-reader). I have also followed the *Gawain* poet's unpredictable patterning of alliteration, though of course diluting those patterns as I have diluted the overall total of alliteration.

There are, to be sure, additional considerations involved in my decision. *Sesed*, "ceased," in line 1, is simply not a workable word for the very first line of a modern English poem—and a poetic translation published in our time must be a modern poem if it is to be anything at all. That is, "ceased" has over the centuries taken on a special, almost Latinate quality that it did not have in the fourteenth century. To automatically carry over *sesed* as "ceased" is therefore to give the poem, from the start, a false flavor, for *Gawain* is verbally (i.e., tonally and rhetorically) consistent. So, too, must its translation be, even if that consistency—in Modern English—requires modification of some individual words. "Ceased" would of course offer a third opportunity for alliteration in line 1. One balances each consideration against others, line by line, situation by situation. In the end, verbal consistency seemed to me, here, more important than alliteration.

There is no way to reproduce *brittened, brent, brondez*, for the key word, *brittened*, "destroyed," is no longer available. I therefore borrowed the poet's own regular reliance on rhyme, in the bob and wheel, and momentarily deviated from alliteration into internal rhyme, employing "smashed / ashes." This internal rhyme is of course entirely my responsibility, but it provides at least a marker of craft-concern, something to alert the modern reader, accustomed to poems for the most part in free verse metric, that the original of this translation-poem works differently. One does what one can, given the conditions and the audience with which one works—both of which are givens, plainly, and not subject to anyone's dictates.

In line 3, I could readily lay on the alliteration, to make it obvious even to an untutored reader that alliteration *mattered* in this poem. I seized the opportunity with relish.

In line 4, again, a key alliterative word, *trewest*, is not properly available in Modern English. In *Gawain* it means "most certain,

surest," which is simply not its modern meaning. (A false friend is
a false friend is a false friend.) Further, the poet says that the traitor
was *tried* (pronounced something like "tree-ed" but having the
modern meaning of "tried"). But this does not tell the background
story that the modern reader needs to know. *Gawain*'s readers and
hearers seem to have known the legend of Aeneas's exile. We do
not, and so I had to tell it, had to explain for what Aeneas was tried
("for Achilles's death") and what the resulting sentence was ("was
exiled"). These may be regrettable necessities, though I do not so
regard them. But they seem plainly necessities: the modern reader
cannot possibly know all that the fourteenth-century reader knew.
But the modern reader must know enough to make ready sense of
what he reads. Excessive reliance on the exact words of a medieval
original, as I indicated in discussing the mead-hall bench phrase of
Beowulf, may seem at first glance to be pure faithfulness, high and
innocent. But it is nothing of the sort. It is, instead, pure pedantry,
and poetry's deadly enemy. Scholars, after all, who can and who do
read poems like *Beowulf* and *Gawain* in the original, neither need
translations nor need to be told of those poems' underlying contexts, their historical backgrounds, and the like. Untutored modern
readers (and for what other class of readers are translations made?)
need to be helped over the endless series of humps and bumps that
the scholar traverses without a second thought.

In lines 6 and 7, I have, for the moment, dropped alliteration.
The modern ear cannot, as I have said, take quite so much of it as
the fourteenth-century regional ear could manage. Equally important, *patrounes* does not mean "patrons," but "lords." And *depreced,*
"subjected," is a word no longer available to us. We can if we
choose say "well nigh," for *welneghe,* but even more obviously than
with *cesed* the word has decisively changed its orientation. "Well
nigh" is colloquial—British and sometimes New England. But *Gawain* is emphatically not a colloquial poem, and must not be made
to appear like one. Q.E.D. *Wele,* "wealth, riches," is also a word no
longer available to us. "Weal," which my desk dictionary defines as
"well-being, prosperity, or happiness," is not the same word as *wele*
(pronounced something like "whale-a"). And "weal" is today a
word of exceedingly limited use—an odd word. *Gawain* is neither
an odd poem nor is it a poem composed of odd words. One cannot
so traduce a helpless older poet.

And there is more to my decision, in these lines, not to allit-
erate. A more important aspect of translation, here and elsewhere,
is as I have said the categorical imperative that the modern poem,

the translation, make sense to a modern reader. (For the record, I quickly go back to alliterating, in line 8, which in my translation reads "And rich: high-handed Romulus made Rome. . . .") Lines 6 and 7 in my translation are no more basic to the poem as a whole than is the poet's whole historical introduction. But for what it may be worth, the poet placed this introduction at the head of his poem, and his readers deserve at least the consideration of being permitted to understand what it says, if not completely to share in the now long-forgotten aura of its associations. The translator cannot fully take his modern reader back into the fourteenth century. He is a translator, neither a science-fiction mechanic working a poetic time machine nor a scholar whose consistent focus necessarily is the fourteenth rather than the twentieth century. But he must be consistently a responsible translator, with his eye forever on his reader's needs.

The *Gawain* poet's high style, which is much French-influenced, is not so easily dealt with. This is not simply a matter of vocabulary borrowings, though in fact roughly one-third of the words used in *Gawain* are of French origin. But all Middle English poets borrowed French words and French approaches and French themes. Some, like John Gower, wrote a good deal of their work in French. Some, like Geoffrey Chaucer, translated French poems. The influence of French language and literature is a general feature of the fourteenth-century poetic landscape in England. What is special, and individual, and difficult about the *Gawain* poet's use of his French peers and predecessors is the unusual combination of native approaches and French ones, the unusual combination of high and low, of religious feeling and of secular feeling, of drama and of irony. Or, in short, what is unique about the work of the *Gawain* poet is that it is unique. And uniqueness is always difficult to translate.

Two brief passages will help indicate the problem. First, the opening lines of the poem's fourth and last section—and two lines will be sufficient:

Now neghez the Nw Yere, and the nyght passez,
The day dryuez to the derk, as Dryghten biddez; . . .

Now New Year's comes, and the night passes,
Daylight replaces darkness, as God
Decrees.

The vocabulary, here, and the treatment, are far closer to Old English than to anything French. The use of the Old English word for "God," *Dryghten,* carries immense historical associations. *Passez* is of course French, but words like *derk* and *neghez, nyght* and *biddez,* thoroughly submerge any non-native influence in a thoroughly English tide.

But in the poem's second section, as Gawain armors himself for his dangerous voyage in search of the green knight, things are portrayed very differently—both in vocabulary and in style:

> When he watz hasped in armes, his harnays watz ryche,
> The lest lachet other loupe lemed of golde.
> So harnayst as he watz he herknez his masse,
> Offred and honoured at the heghe auter.
>
> And Gawain's gear shone rich, the smallest
> Laces and loops glowing with gold.
> Ready in armor, he stood at the altar
> For mass to be chanted . . .

The translator's problem, in handling these divergent passages, is to ensure that each sounds both like itself and like the other. That is, the sense of differentness must not be lost, but so too must the sense of sameness be preserved—as indeed both are maintained in the original. One procedure is to intensify somewhat the alliteration in the first and more Old English–like passage, while lightening and varying it in the more French passage. Another tack is to slightly smooth out the linguistic differences, leaning neither on the *Dryghten* (Old English) sorts of vocabulary, in the first passage, nor on the *offred* and *honoured* (French) vocabulary in the second passage.

That is, the translator must work toward a linguistic and stylistic harmony in his translation, a harmony that parallels but neither completely reflects nor is completely dictated by the linguistic and stylistic features of the original. That unique moment in which the *Gawain* poet wrote is gone, vanished forever. Our Modern English modes, in vocabulary and in style, simply cannot hope to recreate entirely what has left us for good. The translator's task, uncomfortable and perhaps untenable, is to emerge somehow with as much as is capturable in today's English—which is all he has to work with.

So, too, with what was for me the hardest part of the translation, creating an approximation of the original's verse movement and, especially, its wonderfully wrought but absolutely unique texture. The brief passage in which Gawain hears a grindstone, whirring away, sharpening a blade meant for his own neck, is typical:

> Quat! hit clatered in the clyff, as hit cleue schulde,
> As one vpon a gryndelston hade grounden a sythe.
> What! hit wharred and whette, as water at a mulne;
> What! hit rusched and ronge, rawthe to here.

It is not simply that Modern English quite lacks the capacity to make the sounds of this vigorous verse. It is also that the *Gawain* poet is here playing—with us and with his hero. Gawain's horror is meant to be both real and yet also amusing; Gawain's fear is thus meant to be revelatory; and the whole passage is as delicately ironic as it is fearsomely loud and boisterous. How render all of this in Modern English? One does one's best:

> What! It clattered on the cliff, as if
> To split it, like a grindstone grinding a scythe.
> What! It whirred like water at a mill.
> What! It rushed and it rang, and it sang
> Miserably.

Texture is almost everything, in a passage of this sort. And though I have plainly used a good deal of alliteration (though a bit less than in the original), I have also once again dipped into Modern English's bag of rhyme tricks. (Of course, rhyme is also part of the French poet's bag of tricks, and is used by the *Gawain* poet himself in his bob-and-wheel passages.) "Cliff/if," rhyming internally in the first line, is then echoed by "split," in the second line. "Rang/sang" in the fourth line also falls back on internal rhyme, in an attempt to weave the texture closer, tighter. And I have deliberately employed enjambment, placing the important word "miserably" on a separate line, though *rawthe*, "grievous," is not enjambed in the original. The *Gawain* poet's reader-audience surely got the point at once. The sheer exuberance of the description alerted him to its facetiousness—and also to its significance, for this axe-sharpening scene, too, is part of Gawain's testing, and as with the other tests this is one he will partially pass and partially fail. I very much doubt that *everything* experienced by the original reader-audience can possibly be re-created for twentieth-century readers (even if we were at all points absolutely sure just what that original reaction was). But placing "miserably" on a separate line at least highlights, for the modern reader, the peculiar ambivalence Gawain feels, hopefully even reminding that modern reader of the earlier tests and the acute discomfort Gawain experienced at those times, too. It is not precisely the emphasis of the original. But then, the translation is not and never will be the original: that is simply a fact of life.

A rather different example occurs when Gawain, traveling through the wilderness toward his appointment with the green knight, is first received at the castle of the gracious knight Bercilak. (Bercilak later turns out to be the green knight in his untransformed state—but that is not here germane.)

> A cheyer byfore the chemne, ther charcole brenned,
> Watz graythed for Sir Gawan graythely with clothez,
> Whyssynes vpon queldepoyntes that koynt wer bothe;
> And thenne a mere mantyle watz on that mon cast
> Of a broun bleeaunt, enbrauded ful ryche
> And faye furred wythinne with fellez of the best,
> Alle of ermyn in erde, his hode of the same;
> And he sete in that settel semlych ryche,
> And achufed him chefly, and thenne his cher mended.

> In front of the fireplace, where coals glowed,
> They set him a covered chair, its cushions
> Quilted and beautifully worked, embroidered
> In silk; and a brown mantle, richly
> Sewn, and bright, and a gay cloak
> Furred with the thickest skins, was thrown
> On his shoulders; his hood, too, was ermine;
> And Gawain sat in that splendid place
> And soon was warm, and his spirits rose.

The passage is thick with French-derived words, naturally. Scenes of rich and mighty folk naturally lapsed into French vocabulary: the very objects in such settings had French and only French names. But what is chiefly difficult about translating passages like this is the combination of a long, sweeping verse movement and a dense, deeply specific substance. The poet wants us to see and feel and understand the heft and shine of each of the objects he lingers on. But at the same time he wants us to go trippingly through the passage, to get first into other such passages, all richly detailed and all dashing forward, and then into more narrative scenes (all of them having, to be sure, much the same combination of intense detail and forward sweep).

To some extent, alliteration must be lightened in translating these passages. Foot-stomping of a Beowulfian variety does not lend itself to forward speed. But I have tried, at least, to weave alliteration's net—no matter how lightened—across a multiplicity of lines. "Coals," "covered," "cushions," "quilted" run across not one but the first three lines, here (aided and abetted by "glowed," in the first line, and what might be called the "eye alliteration" of "chairs" in the second line). So, too, the third line has "beautifully," "embroidered," the fourth line has "brown," and the fifth line has "bright." This sort of alliterative distribution is definitely not the pattern used by the *Gawain* poet. But, one hopes, it keeps the notion of alliteration spinning through these lines, thus helping to preserve the internal consistency of both form and approach that any translation requires. And, again, it is intended to permit the lines to spin lightly forward, as (or something like) their rapid forward motion in the Middle English original. The syntax, too, is of course deeply reflective of the original. These nine lines have only one full stop and are broken, in the Tolkien-Gordon-Davis text I have used in making the translation, by two semicolons. My translation similarly uses one full stop and three semicolons—the third semicolon marking the difference between the run-on structure of Middle English generally and our Modern English inclination to separate out phrases like *his hode of the same*.

The bob and wheel presented difficulties more narrowly technical. After six hundred years of stress-and-syllable metric in English, and more than six hundred years of rhyming, no modern poet could (or should) experience serious problems with rhyming iambic lines. But fitting the usually very compact sense of those lines into a fixed meter and a tight rhyme scheme, while simultaneously preserving the correct linguistic and stylistic tone, is not always easy. Variations become necessary, since sense must come first, and literal fidelity to form must sometimes bow to it. Not break, but bow: a variant meter or a variant rhyme scheme is not at all the same thing as no meter or no rhyme scheme. Here is the third bob and wheel, in both the original and the translation:

For al watz this fayre folk in her first age,
    on sille,
the hapnest vnder heuen,
Kyng hyghest non of wylle;
Hit were now gret nye to neuen
So hardy a here on hille.

It was springtime in Camelot, in the Christmas snow,
    In that castle
Most blessed on earth,
With the best of vassals
And a king of such worth
That no time will surpass him.

Camelot is of course not specified: this is, however, the court of
King Arthur. Nor does the *Gawain* poet say "springtime" in so
many words. *In her first age,* however, means both in the springtime and in the springtime of their lives—yet another reason, given
the associations of Camelot, for introducing that magical name
into the translation. *On sille* means "in the hall" rather than "in that
castle"—but rhyme too must be permitted its imperatives. The *Gawain* poet says *vnder heuen,* and I turn it 180 degrees, yet with the
same exact meaning: "on earth." Similar and even sharper distortions are enforced by the meter-and-rhyme necessities. "The king
was the greatest man in temper (mind)," says the *Gawain* poet. "In
these days it would be hard to name so bold a company of retainers
(warriors) in any castle." It is not hard to see how these rather
conventional sentiments got themselves reshaped in the translation.
No harm seems to me to have been done, any more than the bob
and wheel itself is damaged, elsewhere, by minor variations in both
meter and rhyme. It is the *fact* of the bob and wheel that matters,
its strange juxtaposition of two traditions. The details, again, strike
me as vastly less significant, certainly for the modern reader,
who needs only to know that a poet who does not write the bulk
of his poem in meter and rhyme does suddenly turn to those devices at the end of each of his poem's sections. That contrast is the
effect I think the translation must aim for. Perfect matching of
meter or rhyme is neither required nor usually desirable: too much
must be given up, and, as I will explain in a moment, even when
metrical identity seems to be achieved it is not achieved, for no
meter in one language is ever identical to a meter in another language.

BARNES & NOBLE #1881

504 RT 17 - (201) 986-1600

REG#03	CLERK 027	RECEIPT#	14459

05/24/93   12:16 PM Wd

S 067417978L CULTURE OF REDEMPTION
LIST PRICE: 14.95   1 @ 13.45   13.45

S 1566191661 1066 & ALL THAT
1 @ 6.98   6.98

S 022604869L CRAFT OF TRANSLATION
LIST PRICE: 8.95   1 @ 8.05   8.05

SUBTOTAL	28.48
SALES TAX - 6%	1.71
TOTAL	30.19

MASTER CARD PAYMENT   30.19
ACCOUNT# 5329031521117Ø803   EXP 0195
AUTHORIZATION #000021
CLERK 27

LIST   30.88 SELL   28.48

YOU SAVED   2.40

AMERICA'S COMPLETE DISCOUNT BOOKSTORE

Chrétien de Troyes's *Yvain*, probably composed about 1177, is one of the many French poems that stand high in the background of *Sir Gawain and the Green Knight*. On generic grounds, there is a clear connection between *Beowulf* and *Gawain*. But surely the connection between *Yvain* and *Gawain* is stronger still, not least because both are Arthurian poems and Chrétien is the Ur-father of that entire huge genre.

But *Yvain* does not present the translator with anything like the problems that *Gawain* does. One must know Old French vocabulary and syntax, to be sure, and neither is always quite so firm and certain as either scholars or translators would like. But once past the merely linguistic hurdles (and those hurdles are always made far too much of in what nontranslators write about the art of translation), *Yvain* is an astonishingly modern poem, full of bright, witty dialogue, brilliant description, acute psychological insight, marvellous narration, keen sociological awareness, and a delightful overall pragmatic realism. Chrétien is a dashing, sometimes bawdy realist, and he is literarily incredibly consistent. There is none of the insistent defensiveness of *Beowulf*, none of the layer-upon-layer complexity, the mingling of times and styles and approaches to be found in *Gawain*. In those respects, turning *Yvain* into modern English is a joy and a delight, hardly a task at all.

The principal problem is the formal one. Chrétien writes in octosyllabic couplets—syllable-counted couplets, of course, since Old French is still French, not English. These couplets rhyme. And there are both historical and literary reasons for Chrétien's choice of such a swift-moving, partially oral-oriented form. There were undoubtedly those who read his work off the page, perhaps even silently, perhaps simply to themselves. But most of the time *Yvain* would have been read aloud, often by the poet himself, and the audience would not have had a written text in front of them. Their ears would have been their only guide. (Whether everyone in such an audience would have been able to follow a printed text is another question.)

A formal measure of some sort is of course required for the translation of *Yvain*. Free verse is a fine enough measure, in its place, but a twelfth-century courtly romance is simply not where it belongs. The immediate assumption, made in fact by some translators of Chrétien (and of *Yvain*), is that octosyllabic in Old French equals tetrameter in Modern English. It is a deadly as well as an erroneous assumption. No meter in any language, no matter how

closely that language may resemble another language, is so simply
and mechanically transportable. I have tried, for the sake of the
experiment, to render German iambics into English iambics and
the effect is both incredibly unlike the effect of the original and
incredibly bad as English poetry. In my *Art of Translating Poetry*, I
try to explain in suitable detail why no metric can ever be translated
literally (any more than words can be).[6] Each meter accomplishes
in one language what no other meter can, either in that language
or in any other. Again, it is the *effect* at which the translator who
employs metrical forms must aim, not the envelope in which that
effect is contained.

Additionally, any competent poet knows that in Modern English iambic tetrameter is suitable only for very short poems. If the
translator of a poem is not himself a competent poet, plainly he
ought not attempt to translate a poem. At lengths greater than, say,
forty or fifty lines, iambic tetrameter turns into a deadly bore—to
which fact the bulk of the poetry written by AE (George William
Russell) bears vivid if melancholy witness.

The translator of *Yvain* is therefore forced, like the translator
of any ancient poem, to consider how best to devise a formal equivalent, workable in his own tradition, for the formal devices the
older poet used in his poem. English is a stress-timed language;
French is syllable-timed. We can say, and we sometimes do, that the
twelve-syllable alexandrine is roughly the equivalent of iambic pentameter (which usually has ten syllables). But the equation is by no
means perfect or invariable, and it is of no application whatever to
other sorts of metrics, either French or English. What Chrétien
wanted, in *Yvain*, was a relatively short line, one that moved
quickly enough to sustain his swift narrative pace and his charming
inventiveness. Not only does iambic tetrameter not accomplish
this, it positively militates against it, being an intrinsically faintly
passive measure, suitable for poetry like A. E. Housman's, or for
Matthew Prior's dry musings, but hardly workable in a fast-
moving narrative poem of almost seven thousand lines.

Being familiar with the native Old English tradition, as well as
with its later developments, I opted for a fairly short stress-timed
line, having three clear stresses and whatever number of unstressed
syllables might be necessary. No such line has to my knowledge

---

6. Burton Raffel, *The Art of Translating Poetry* (University Park: Pennsylvania
State University Press, 1988), pp. 80–94.

ever been used in English—but then, no one has succeeded in translating *Yvain* into good, readable English verse. Further: rhyme was an oral-based device in Chrétien's time, necessary in the context of his poem's public performances. And French, as everyone knows, is far richer in rhyme than is English—a fact which hardly escaped the attention of John Milton. Rhyme was necessary, in Chrétien's time and in Chrétien's language. It would be a distraction rather than an ornament in a Modern English translation. Something would be lost, to be sure, by dropping the rhyme. But even more would be gained.

I was not especially confident of these formal decisions, at the start of things. I sent a sample of the projected translation to a number of qualified people, asking them all the same questions: Does this sound like Chrétien? Does this move like Chrétien? Will this formal solution work through *Yvain*'s almost seven thousand lines? The answers, rather to my surprise, were uniformly positive—though one respondent, to her credit, demanded to see a larger sample before passing on the question of verse movement. (I subsequently sent her a sample of some hundreds of lines, and she then pronounced the solution workable.)

The proof of the pudding, of course, is in the eating. Here then are some samples:[7]

Il avint, pres a de set anz,
Que je seus come paisanz
Aloie querant avantures,
Armez de totes armeures
Si come chevaliers doit estre,
Et trovai un chemin a destre
Parmi une forest espesse.

It was almost seven years
Ago, I was lonely as a peasant
And hunting after adventure,
Fully armed, exactly
As a knight ought to be, and I came
To a road on my right-hand side,
In the middle of a deserted forest.

7. Chrétien de Troyes, *Yvain*, translated by Burton Raffel (New Haven: Yale University Press, 1987), pp. 8, 135.

Perhaps because Chrétien uses many polysyllabic words, and undercuts his rhymes by continuous enjambment, I think the effect in the translation is reasonably close to that of the original. A more active passage may provide a still better test:

> De priiere aie li font
> Les dames; qu'autre bastons n'ont.
> Et li lions li fet aie
> Tel, qu'a la premiere anvaie
> A de si grant air feru
> Le seneschal, qui a pié fu,
> Que aussi, con ce fussent pailles,
> Fet del hauberc voler les mailles,
> Et contrevai si fort le sache,
> Que de l'espaule li esrache
> Le tandron atot le costé.

> Having no other weapons,
> The ladies helped with their prayers.
> And the lion brought him different
> Assistance, leaping so fiercely
> At the steward, who was fighting on foot,
> Attacking so furiously that he scattered
> The mail from his armor like so much
> Straw, and seizing him in his jaws
> Dragged him down so viciously
> That he ripped the flesh from his shoulder
> All along his side.

I have noted, earlier, that a poem of 3,182 lines (*Beowulf*) took me six months to draft, and a poem of 2,530 lines (*Gawain*) took me eighteen months to draft. *Yvain* is a poem of 6,818 lines, or more than twice the length of *Beowulf*, but it still took me only six months to draft. Once I had solved the formal problem, there were virtually no others.

As I said at the start, I am not so much avoiding larger generalizations as desperately trying to contain them. I do not believe that any good-sized medieval poem, in any European language, or from any part of the medieval period, can be approached or translated exactly like any other good-sized medieval poem. The three such poems that I have myself translated have all presented unique opportunities and unique problems. Indeed, the shortest of them, *Sir*

Gawain and the Green Knight, was without question the hardest for me to translate, and the longest, *Yvain,* was incomparably the easiest. (I suspect this would hold true for all of Chrétien's work, but I have not yet attempted to prove the point.) It seems reasonably clear that the closeness of Chrétien's inner world to our modern inner world is one of the basic underlying factors, if not *the* single most important factor, explaining these facts. We are not at all close to the inner world of *Beowulf,* but it at least presents a unified, rock-solid consistency. *Gawain*'s inner world is split in at least half a dozen different directions, bifurcated, uncertain, always in transition. The literary effect of *Gawain* is consistent, to be sure, because its author was a great poet. But the road to that consistency is a fearfully tangled one for the translator, as in all probability it was for the original poet, too.

If then there is any overarching lesson to be learned from my remarks, it is, as I have argued many times before, that the literary translator is necessarily engaged with far more than words, far more than techniques, far more than stories or characters or scenes. He is—and the literary translator of medieval works is even more deeply so—engaged with worldviews and with the passionately held inner convictions of men and women long dead and vanished from the earth. A large part of his task, and perhaps the most interesting (once he acquires essential but merely preliminary technical skills), is the mining out and reconstruction of those worldviews, those passionately held and beautifully embodied inner convictions. I am deeply convinced that it is precisely this that keeps me, after something like twenty volumes of verse translation, looking forward to more.

COLLABORATION, REVISION, AND OTHER LESS FORGIVABLE SINS IN TRANSLATION
EDMUND KEELEY

There was a time when translators and translating were so marginal to the world of letters, so undervalued and underpaid, that a chauvinistic defense of the craft before any audience that might listen seemed not simply a matter of redressing injustice but a demonstration of commitment essential for survival. That time now appears to have passed: these days translators are more in than they are out. And this means that one can now take a more relaxed approach in commenting on the craft of translation, even attempt to tell one's share of the whole truth—anyway that part of it that long experience tends to verify.

My experience compels me to say at the start that any discussion of translation in broad terms is dangerous, and any discussion of the craft of translation by an individual translator—though less dangerous and perhaps finally more valuable—has to be as subjective and limited as, say, that of an individual poet commenting on the craft of poetry or a novelist on the craft of fiction. My sense of the danger in generalizing about translation can be illustrated by two of the most common generalizations that one hears: namely, that translation is a betrayal (*traduttore e traditore*) and that what constitutes poetry is exactly what is lost when poetry is translated into another language (ascribed to Robert Frost). There is a half truth in both of these general propositions. The other half truth is their reverse image, equally valid, equally false. Some would say that translation, far from being a betrayal, is in fact a salvation, bringing to the translated text the kind of long life it could not possibly have in the original alone, especially when the original is in an obscure language. And in the second instance, some would say—Ezra Pound and W. H. Auden perhaps among these—that what constitutes poetry, at least in the individual case, is exactly what survives in translation: that which is so essentially poetic in a given poet's voice that it can be heard in any translation, for ex-

Edmund Keeley is a novelist and professor of English and creative writing at Princeton University. He has translated works by C. P. Cavafy, Angelos Sikelianos, George Seferis, Odysseus Elytis, Yannis Ritsos, and Vassilis Vassilikos. He has also written several critical studies of modern Greek poetry.

ample, what Auden calls Cavafy's "unique tone of voice," unmistakable in English, he believes, whoever the translator may be.

So much for generalities and their partial access to truth, an indulgence that the practicing translator can usually avoid simply by keeping his mind on the difficult work in front of him, thereby restricting space for abstract thought about the implications of what he is up to. But since I have been given the task of writing about practice rather than theory, I feel a responsibility to say something truthful about my experience in the workshop, which has often included another practitioner working beside me, and this sometimes over a long spread of years. I can see both strength and weakness in such long-term collaboration, and having recently decided to work for the most part on my own from now on, a review of my collaborative practice—a kind of taking stock in this area—may be useful for the record as an example of one approach to the craft, even if still a personal case.

My principal collaboration has been in the translation of poetry, and my principal collaborator in this genre has been the British poet and scholar, Philip Sherrard (I have also collaborated on occasion with my wife, Mary—though our most extended effort was in fiction—and I have also worked on two volumes of poetry with the Greek editor and critic George Savidis). The collaboration with Sherrard was initially the product of convenience more than anything else. At the time I had barely accepted the idea that translation was a truly creative enterprise. True creativity meant poetry, fiction, and plays, though I was prepared to think of translation as a pleasurable necessity, especially if one was interested in promoting the masterworks of an unrecognized culture, as I then regarded, with some justification, the culture of modern Greece. What I had in mind specifically was bringing together several of the important modern Greek poets—Cavafy, Sikelianos, Seferis, Elytis for a start—in a volume of English translations that would do better justice to those poets who had already been rendered into English and serve to introduce others who had not. I had read some translations of C. P. Cavafy by Philip Sherrard in an early 1950s issue of *Encounter,* and these had impressed me as the finest English versions of that poet I had come across, certainly more contemporary and less stilted than many of the pioneer versions— in particular, the rhymed versions by John Mavrogordato that had first brought this marvelous Alexandrian voice and sensibility into the English-speaking world in a relatively complete rendering. I had some Cavafy translations of my own, but more of Seferis and Elytis, and a few by lesser poets. It seemed to me foolish to duplicate the good work that Sherrard had already done: my ambition wasn't to challenge other translators but to find a way for more of the best contemporary Greek poetry in current versions to reach an audience in America and England than had managed to do so at that time. So I sought out Sherrard to learn whether we might somehow share in an anthology for this purpose.

It turned out that Sherrard was vacationing with his family and several friends on the island of Thassos, offshore from the Macedonian town of Kavalla (this was the summer of 1956, as I remember). It was saint's day at one of the island's high, inland churches, and that was where the men in Sherrard's group—another Englishman and a South African—were headed when my wife and I tracked them down. What followed for me was a British "walk" of some hours at a fast pace mostly uphill to the chosen village square, the occasional brief pausing on the way simply to allow the American, youngest of the company, to catch up every now and then so that he wouldn't get totally discouraged and stray from the true path. The collaboration with Sherrard was finally sealed just before midnight with a second bottle of raki. Sherrard was to provide his Cavafy and a selection of Sikelianos, and I was to add to this my Seferis, Elytis, and whatever else we determined was worthy from other translations he and I had on hand. And we decided simply to split the work of introducing the poets by way of a critical preface.

The agreement held firm even after more sober reflection, and several years later—neither of us was in any great hurry—we met on the island of Evia, north of Athens, to put our contributions together and to write the joint introduction. What emerged was *Six Poets of Modern Greece,* published in England by Thames and Hudson in 1960 and in the United States by Alfred Knopf in 1961. I now find the method of that volume remarkable in its casualness. It was largely a matter of our bringing together what both of us had ready, my adding a bit to Sherrard's Cavafy and Sikelianos, his adding a bit to my Seferis and Elytis, his agreeing to include the few poems by Gatsos and Antoniou that I had attempted, sharing the decision not to spend any more time, given the years that had already gone by, exploring other possibilities such as Kariotakis, whom we both knew to a degree, or Ritsos, whom we hardly knew at all.

We did of course read each other's work, but in this first collaboration diplomacy dominated criticism, so that few alterations emerged during our job of pasting together a more or less coherent, if hardly representative, anthology. We had to count on whatever qualities each of us brought individually to the texts that were finally included, and the difference in voice between us—evident most glaringly in what I could later discern as certain Britishisms or Americanisms—became part of the difference in voice between the various poets included. I can also discern two rather distinct styles in the critical introduction, though here we did allow ourselves a certain amount of fiddling with each other's syntax to provide for a fairly neutral texture in that regard at least.

Is such casualness to be thought of as sinful? That would depend on one's position regarding integrity of voice in translation. One position at the extreme is that the translator's voice should show clearly in the translated text, as a poet's voice—if it is to have any claim to distinction—surely must show in the poetry he writes. And a position at the other extreme—humility the virtue here—is that the finest translators do what they can to mute their own voice so that the reader presumably has a better chance of hearing whatever can be rendered of the original poet's voice. Sherrard and I did not take a position; we simply published whatever voice each of us separately had fashioned in those particular renderings at that particular time. If there was sin in this, it was unpremeditated.

There was considerably more premeditating in the case of our second collaboration almost a decade later. The circumstances were different. In this instance we had a single poet to deal with, George Seferis, and a large body of work: all that he had published over a period of thirty years. And the poet was still alive; in fact, Sherrard and I had both come to know him well enough by that time to call him a friend. Some might see an immediate advantage in having the poet one is translating alive and friendly, perhaps enough so to become a third party to the collaboration; and others, perhaps more skeptical or sagacious from some personal experience, would see great dangers in such a triangle. Seferis deliberately chose not to become involved in our work, at least not overtly. He said his English was not good enough. But his sometimes heavy shadow was always behind us in our work, or so I felt. And just to remind us that his English wasn't all that bad, the poet would occasionally send a postcard from his latest diplomatic outpost—Ankara, Beirut, Amman—correcting this or that mistranslation of a word or phrase in the latest prepublication offprint to reach his desk. And another circumstance: Sherrard and I had both been away from translating for some years, our devotion given to other kinds of writing, so that we perhaps felt that we could afford to be more humble regarding the translation at hand. In any case, that is what I think we chose to be.

I do not remember actually discussing how we ought to approach the Collected Seferis, as we called the work-in-progress. I suspect that our approach emerged from the strategy we adopted for the volume. We decided to divide up the Greek edition of Seferis' work quite arbitrarily, poem by poem, without any consideration for private preferences, though each of us took initial responsibility for particular poems that each had already translated. It was a kind of lottery at this first stage, an attempt to encourage the eventual development of a unified, neutral voice for Seferis in English. Since we lived in different countries, the collaboration was mostly by mail. I would send Sherrard, then living in England, drafts of my assigned poems for his review, and he would send me drafts of his. We would take each other's comments into account as we chose and then send out a second draft for review. Finally, in the summers, we would meet in a village by the sea in Evia, where Sherrard had settled with his family for his days in Greece, and where my wife and I eventually bought a piece of land, and we would sit down at a table with Parnassus in the distance across the gulf to read the draft translations aloud to each other and work on them intensely until they sounded right.

We did not much discuss what "right" meant, except to agree that any idioms too specifically British or American should be avoided, along with all archaisms, inversions, personal idiosyncrasies, and rhetorical flourishes that might make Seferis sound less frugal, less demotic and contemporary, than he sounded in Greek. In short, we worked mostly from whatever our training and instinct gave us as writers in English, much as we would separately in other creative work, but with a critic at hand whose opinion carried particular weight. Our knowledge of Greek proved to balance out, Sherrard having a stronger traditional base through his specialization in classical and medieval Greek, I a stronger grasp of the range of contemporary idiom as a result of my several childhood and postadolescent years in Greece. At this stage of the collaboration there were disagreements, compromises, a sometimes haunting sense of inadequacy that would push us to debate the sound of a phrase or line even after heading out to sea in a casual matching sidestroke during the heat of the afternoon or during the evening's bout with densely resinated wine at the local taverna. But by the end of the summer sessions it was no longer easy to know who had done the first draft of what poem, and by the time the book went to press, after further revision in proof, impossible—to my ear at least. It seemed to me that our voice for Seferis in English was there.

What was not quite there to the degree it might have been even in translation was Seferis's Greek voice, though we didn't get around to admitting this to ourselves for more than another decade, when a new expanded edition of the Collected Seferis was solicited by Princeton University Press. In the meanwhile there had been more Evian summers devoted to the Collected Cavafy that we brought out in 1975 and the Selected Sikelianos that we brought out in 1979. Our turning to Cavafy brought special problems into the collaboration and at least two particular solutions. Before taking on the whole of the Alexandrian poet we decided, in 1972, to offer a selection of his work in a version that seemed to us to liberate him from both the prosy dryness and the various kinds of poetizing evident in the translations then on the market, including some of the lines in our own *Six Poets* selection. Our impulse was to bring Cavafy into the post-sixties by creating a voice for him that we hoped would sound as contemporary as the best Anglo-American poetry of the day. As we put it in the Foreword to that volume, we were motivated by "a growing sense that Cavafy should be rendered in a style that is neither stilted nor artificial"; we had reached the conclusion, during our twenty-odd years of familiarity with his poetry, that "his voice is more natural, immediate, and even colloquial than extant translations—including our own earlier selections—would make it appear" and that his Greek, "even with its deliberate archaisms, is closer in crucial ways to the spoken idiom than is the language of other leading Greek poets of his time." So our language was to be appropriately colloquial, devoid of all archaisms—since the poet's own could not be approximated in English with anything like the same effect—and our new renderings would make "no attempt to reproduce Cavafy's sporadic rhyme schemes and syntactical idiosyncrasies" because any such attempt would lead to "artificiality or pedantic literalness," especially grave sins, we felt, in poems predominantly dramatic.

This perhaps too self-conscious effort to update Cavafy can be illustrated by a few lines from our different versions of two of his

best-known poems, "Waiting for the Barbarians" and "The City."
The opening lines of the first read as follows in our early *Six Poets*
version:

> What are we waiting for, gathered in the market-place?
>
> The barbarians are to arrive today.
>
> Why so little activity in the Senate?
> Why do the Senators sit there without legislating?
>
> Because the barbarians will arrive today.
> Why should the Senators bother with laws now?
> The barbarians, when they come, will do the law-making.

In the Selected Cavafy of a decade later, this has become:

> What are we waiting for, packed in the forum?
>
> The barbarians are due here today.
>
> Why isn't anything going on in the senate?
> Why have the senators given up legislating?
>
> Because the barbarians are coming today.
> What's the point of senators and their laws now?
> When the barbarians get here, they'll do the legislating.

Our updating both in the market-place/forum and in the senate
is apparent from the syntax and the diction, the colloquial tone
perhaps closer to the right one for a dialogue between the man in
the street and his companion watching the mysterious doings of
those who govern them more or less. But "packed" can be seen as
overloading the Greek "*synathrismeni*" ("gathered together") with
anachronistic connotations picked up in modern trains and football
stadiums. And the early "Why so little activity in the Senate?"
though a bit more stilted than the later "Why isn't anything going
on in the senate?" now seems a degree closer to Cavafy's "mia tetia
apraxia" ("such inactivity") in his capitalized "*Singlito.*"
      The second example illustrates a hesitancy that was generated
by the distortion that has accompanied every attempt—anyway, so

far—to rhyme Cavafy in English: distortion sometimes gilded by dubious music. Here is the first stanza of "The City" in the *Six Poets* version, which we rhymed as strictly as Cavafy's poem:

> You said: "I shall go to another land, go to another sea.
> Another town shall be found better than this one.
> Ill-starred and vain is all I have ever done,
> and my heart—like a dead body—within me is entombed.
> For how long is my mind to this marasmus doomed?
> Wherever I turn my eyes, if I gaze no matter where,
> the black ruins of my life I see, here,
> where so many years have I spent, destroyed, wasted utterly."

And the Selected Cavafy version:

> You said: "I'll go to some other place, some other sea,
> find another city better than this one.
> Every move I make is doomed to come out wrong
> and my heart, like something dead, lies buried inside me.
> How long is my mind to wither away like this?
> Wherever I turn, wherever I look,
> I see the black ruin of my life, here,
> where I've spent so many years—wasted, destroyed them utterly."

The virtues gained by our having dropped the rhyming are manifest: "shall be found" vanishes from the second line, "within me is entombed" from the fourth, "this marasmus doomed" from the fifth, the redundancy of "gaze no matter where" in the sixth. And gone is the inversion of the verb in the final line of the stanza—though that was a bit of poetizing that can't be blamed on the necessity of a rhyme. But of course the formal dexterity of the original is lost as well, this missing element commemorated—quite inadvertently, I am certain—by the remnant rhymes in lines 1, 4, and 8, which somehow got in there despite our stated impulse, perhaps an unconscious gesture toward the formalism of the original, perhaps a musical accident.

Our effort to bring Cavafy into the post-sixties world met with a generally warm reception from reviewers, and the translation ended up an unsuccessful finalist for the National Book Award; but it hardly earned total assent, the criticism coming for the most part from those who were actually familiar with the Greek original.

From the perspective of some of those whose primary interest was in Cavafy's Greek text and who felt a need to protect that text—or anyway their image of it—our new version was evidently a bit too jazzy, too essentially colloquial, without demonstrating due respect for Cavafy's varied, idiosyncratic style, which mixed purist and demotic forms freely and sometimes gave syntax and even diction a strictly personal flavor coming out of Alexandria and influenced by Pontic constructions inherited from the poet's Constantinopolitan mother. And then there was our failure to provide any sense of Cavafy's sometimes elaborate and playful rhyming, especially in his earlier verse, before free verse came to dominate his work. All true, but, as one of our most demanding critics put it, all too much to hope for in any single translator's lifetime, or even the lifetime of a collaboration—and this is especially so when one is moving out of an inflected language with an unsettled texture that, in Cavafy's hands, permits the most artificial forms to work beside the most ordinary, both more available to rhyme than the possibilities offered by English.

Still, whatever the merits and demerits of a particular version, if a collaboration is fortunate enough to have a relatively long life, there will always be time for decisions and revisions that a new edition can reverse. By the time Sherrard and I arrived in Evia three years later for work on our Collected Cavafy, either age, or creeping conservatism, or the knowledge that the original Greek would now appear on the page facing our translation—perhaps some combination of these—served to inhibit to a degree our earlier impulse to make Cavafy blatantly modern in English. In several instances we found ourselves returning to our earliest renderings or some equivalent thereof. For example, the opening line of "Waiting for the Barbarians" now reads: "What are we waiting for, assembled in the forum?" the earlier "packed" having gone the way of the even earlier "gathered," presumably because "assembled" has more of the literal "gathered together" in it and thus emphasizes the pseudo-ceremony of the occasion, ordered by the vanishing powers that be. In the case of "The City," the remnant rhyme has been excised, "other place" in the first line has become "country," "wither" now reads "moulder," "utterly" has become "totally," all more or less innocuous changes meant to promote accuracy or naturalness. The two substantial changes are in lines 4 and 7—the first of these the most troublesome line in the poem—where we attempt to simplify an awkward image by the new phrasing "and my heart lies buried like something dead" and, in the second instance, where "the black ruin of my life" becomes "the black ruins of my life" in order to provide a visual image of ruins in Cavafy's desolate city landscape, as in the original Greek.

The impulse in the case of the Collected Cavafy was less that of contemporaneity and more that of accuracy in both substance and tone, and this resulted in a somewhat less colloquial version than that of the Selected Cavafy, but one that is perhaps more in keeping with the mixed linguistic coloring, the play between formal and informal language, that one finds in Cavafy's text. Yet it became characteristic of our collaboration at this time not to regard any of our versions as fixed and final. A later printing of the Collected Cavafy (1980) is labelled "with corrections," and there were a few further "corrections" a year later when Sherrard and I brought out a new anthology to replace our old out-of-print Six Poets volume. It is clear that we continued to be pursued by that troublesome line in "The City," which now reads "and my heart lies buried as though it were something dead," a bit more formal yet. I doubt that it will stay that way. If one believes—as I think Sherrard and I do—that translation is a movable feast that must initially serve the taste of its particular day and then be prepared to change in keeping with the taste of another day, and second, that any single translation of a text is by definition an incomplete and somewhat distorted image of the original, there must always be room for retouching and sharpening that image as new taste and new perception may indicate. And of course this carries with it the danger of expanding rather than diminishing the degree of distortion.

Which brings me back to Seferis and the revision of our work on his poetry. Seferis himself thought it sinful of a poet to alter his own work once the text of a poem had been published and established as part of that poet's canon. He once told me that he found it "inexcusable" that Auden should decide to drop a whole stanza of his "1 September 1939" when it was reprinted in his Collected Shorter Poems, 1930–1944. "Even if your beliefs may change as you grow older, the poem is a work of art that expresses you as you were when you wrote it and therefore has no business changing." I wonder what he felt about the changes over time in the Keeley-Sherrard version of his poetry. While he was alive, he had no comment on that matter or the translation of his poetry in general—except to say at one point that of course our English version, any

English version of his work, was the translator's poetry, not his. That, I suppose, is fair enough. In any case, our collaboration kept producing a slightly different poem every time we had a chance to go at the text anew, and that includes our most recent version, reshaped in the same village on the Evian Gulf during the summer of 1986.

A single example that I have discussed in part elsewhere and that can now be updated will serve for an easily accessible case in point: the opening lines of the opening poem in Seferis's crucial series of twenty-four poems called *Mythistorima*, the volume that helped to bring new possibilities into Greek poetry during the decade of the thirties, much as *The Waste Land* did for Anglo-American poetry during the twenties. The context of the passage in question is an Odyssean journey of discovery and return (or *nostos*) that is never quite fulfilled satisfactorily, neither in this poem nor in the series as a whole, but that begins with a search for "the first seed" so that the contemporary protagonists can again find what they have lost out of their ancient past that might bring new life into their arid present. In this opening poem, "1," they wait for the new beginning through some kind of annunciation:

> For three years
> we waited intently for the messenger
> watching closely
> the pines the shore and the stars.
> One with the plough's blade or the keel of the ship,
> we were searching to find the first seed
> that the ancient drama might begin again.
> We returned to our homes broken,
> our limbs incapable, our mouths ruined
> by the taste of rust and brine . . .

This is how we rendered the poem's first stanza and part of the second stanza in our earliest attempt, published in *Six Poets* as part of the Seferis selection in that volume, third among the six. But when we came to the 1967 Collected Seferis, the poem took on a particular significance because we decided to begin the volume and our own journey through Seferis's collected work with this free verse opening of the *Mythistorima* series rather than with Seferis's earlier rhymed poems, which we placed in an appendix along with some later work that we also did not attempt to offer in rhymed versions. The poem "1" of *Mythistorima* would thus set the tone of the volume and signal the character of our Seferis translation, which is why this poem cost us more labor initially—and indeed in the long run—than any other poem in the Collected Seferis. The first problem we had to solve was that of the first line in the Greek original, consisting of the noun (with its article) "*ton angelo*," which means "the angel" in contemporary usage, connoting first of all a thing good or beautiful or both, as in the phrase "you're an angel." But the 3,000-year history of the Greek language has loaded the word with other nuances out of both the pagan and Christian traditions: the messenger of classical drama and the holy angel of the Old and New Testaments. The protagonists in Seferis's poem are waiting for this image of the good and the beautiful because it will presumably help them find what they are looking for in order to initiate a rebirth of prospects, if not actually a return to their lost paradise, their elusive Ithaca. The figure who appears at the start of the poem is not merely a messenger bringing news of what has happened off-stage; it is primarily an angel capable of some sort of annunciation, a kind of herald. So that is how we chose to name the figure in the Collected Seferis—largely under Sherrard's persuasion—this in contrast to the earlier renderings by all hands, which uniformly favored the term "messenger":

> Three years
> we waited intently for the herald
> closely watching
> the pine the shore and the stars.
> One with the plough's blade or the keel of the ship,
> we were searching to rediscover the first seed
> so that the ancient drama could begin again.

Besides highlighting what seems an annunciation, this version establishes more clearly the implication in the original that the protagonists are engaged in a search not merely to "find" the first seed but to "rediscover" a thing lost so that an old order can come into being anew. So far so good. The trouble with this rendering is that the word "herald" gives the passage a heavily Christian tone that is not entirely consistent with an annunciation meant to signal the rediscovery of a first seed that will allow "the ancient drama" to begin again. And the rendering also fails to convey the dramatic emphasis of Seferis's poem, the setting off of his angel in a single

opening line (though we do make a gesture in that direction by
dropping the "For" of the *Six Poets* version). By the time we were
given a chance to revise and expand the Collected Seferis a decade
or so later, we had decided to sacrifice both ease of syntax and the
pointed Christian nuance in an attempt to represent more effectively the drama of the poet's opening and to offer a more neutral,
more comprehensive figure:

> The angel—
> three years we waited intently for him
> closely watching
> the pines the shore and the stars . . .

After so much vision and revision, it seemed to us that the text
would remain stable as long as we were likely to be watching over
it, but one characteristic of collaboration is, evidently, the doubling
of afterthoughts: one or another of the collaborators is bound to
read some part of the text again and find something there that still
does not sound quite right and, given the existence of a partner in
the enterprise, to feel a moral obligation to communicate his new
hesitancy about that bit of the text. Though Seferis had passed on
by the time of our expanded edition and his gentle shadow no
longer hovered over us—nor the threat of his correspondence from
distant places—we would find ourselves occasionally sending postcards to each other with a suggested alteration of this or that line
in one or another poem by some one of our jointly translated poets.
These suggestions would be duly recorded for further perusal when
we next got together to prepare a new edition or anthology selection.

In the case of Seferis, the opening of *Mythistorima* was allowed
to rest in our 1981 version until an English publisher (Anvil Press)
decided to reset the text for an English-only edition to be distrib-
uted in Britain and the Commonwealth. That permitted a review
of the Collected edition from beginning to end during the summer
of 1986, again in Evia, with renewed agonizing over the opening
lines of the volume. After much debate—much shuffling of syntax
in particular—we settled on a single change that had actually been
anticipated a few years earlier in our revised anthology, called *The
Dark Crystal* in Greece and *Voices of Modern Greece* in the United
States. The last line of the opening stanza now reads: "so that the
primordial drama could begin again." The choice of our original

term, "ancient drama," was no doubt influenced by our joint clas-
sicist prejudices, shared with most other Anglo-American philhel-
lenes. The Greek does not say "*archaio drama*" but "*panarchaio
drama*," which suggests not only pre-Christian but pre-classical ori-
gins, something very ancient, primeval, close to the beginning of
time. That is presumably where a "first seed" would begin its work
of rebirth, well before the days of Aeschylus, Sophocles, and Eurip-
ides.

What conclusions can one draw from this history of our collaboration? It seems to me that we began with very little agreed-
upon conception—anyway, very little verbalized conception—of
what mode of translation we were to offer our readers other than a
rendering governed by what each of us separately thought was a
relevant contemporary voice for the poets we were translating. We
then moved on to a more or less conscious effort to shape an appropriate composite voice for Seferis and Cavafy by commenting
on each other's work extensively and meeting over a period of time
to test the voice by reciting it to ourselves and working on it further. The voice we chose for the Selected Cavafy was the most deliberate, engendered by a view of his work that chose to emphasize
the colloquial element in it and to flatten out both the idiosyncrasies and formal elements in diction and metrical structure, including rhyme. This decision promoted a version in which the translators' voice often appeared to dominate the text, updating it
blatantly at times, to the pleasure of some and the displeasure of
others. Our efforts thereafter took a somewhat different tack. The
impulse remained that of creating a contemporary voice for each
of the poets we turned to—in addition to Cavafy and Seferis, the
more lyrical Sikelianos and Elytis—but we now made a more focused attempt to capture what forgotten nuances in the original we
could uncover even if sometimes too new to the ear for comfort,
to keep the tone more formal at times than persistent colloquialism
allows, to avoid strict equivalents for conventional meters and set
rhyme patterns yet to make some gestures toward paralleling the
original syntax when that served to convey dramatic values insis-
tently there in the original.

Our Selected Sikelianos, a late product of the collaboration
(1979), perhaps best illustrates the strengths and weaknesses of this
final stance. The selection is thin in the light of Sikelianos's broad
oeuvre because we included very few of his long, formally conventional poems, where linguistic and musical values work in the

Greek to keep the poet's large rhetorical predispositions more or
less vital (in English translation there can be no such saving grace),
and we concentrated on those poems that had a mythic, dramatic,
or narrative base to sustain the poet's grand—sometimes grandi-
loquent—first-person voice. In short, our selection was loaded to
permit us to attempt a voice for Sikelianos that would not seem as
flamboyant, strident, or otherwise excessive as a representative selection in English might well have promoted in unpalatable measure. And of course this meant sacrificing some of his more renowned "philosophical" verse, along with a just representation of
his lyricism. On the other hand, this kind of rigorous selection
allowed us to focus our own developing "formalism" more effectively so as to render some of the poems chosen in blank verse or
other metrical equivalents that were stricter than anything we had
so far attempted—and this included a number of unrhymed
though metrically regular renderings of Sikelianos's conventional
sonnets. In the case of this volume, we again divided up the work
arbitrarily at the first-draft stage, but I remember our later meet-
ings to work out a final version as the easiest of our long collaboration. It was as though we had by then settled on the common
voice as translators that had emerged only with harsh effort and
constant testing in earlier years. Whether or not that ease shows in
the published text, I cannot say, but here again I find that I am no
longer able to pick out which translations were originally mine and
which Sherrard's, and that, I hope, serves Sikelianos as one would
want a collaborative effort to do when it is singing in tune and in
the right key.

I suspect that the lighter labor of the Sikelianos volume originated in part from the sympathy of our response to his work, our
agreement before the fact about how important—if often awkward—his generally unrecognized poetry actually was and also
how difficult it would be to convey that importance in English. I
imagine that this sort of sympathy is, finally, the essential require-
ment of a fully productive collaboration. When it is not there in
large measure, the going can be rough. When it is not there at all,
I think collaboration is not only sinful but probably impossible (as
I take it to be the case with Yannis Ritsos, whom I have occasionally translated with other collaborators but for the most part on my
own). Sherrard and I appear to have had exceptional luck in finding
ground for sympathy, considering the diversity of the texts we have
collaborated on over the years. If the vein of poetry we might

choose to work on together is now running thin, I have no doubt
that our commitment to the unstable text and the need for revision
in keeping with our changing perceptions will bring us back together over one or another of our poets—again on the inland shore
of Evia opposite Parnassus, if the gods go on being as good to us
as they have been so far.

PLEASURES AND PROBLEMS OF TRANSLATION
DONALD FRAME

The only kind of translation I want to talk about is what I call "free literary translation," or translation of literature chosen freely by the translator for this purpose. This is the only kind I have much interest in or knowledge of, and I think it is an art, though a very modest minor one, since it requires constant choice by the translator among the author's values and devices as he seeks to recapture them in his own language and finds he can rarely if ever recapture them all. Clearly it belongs far below good literary creation, and below good literary analysis, but I think it demands much of the same sensitivity as both of these, a sensitivity shared by many booklovers whose gifts for good creation or analysis may be modest or nonexistent.

I find it pleasant to see how much of a favorite author you can bring across into your own language. As has been said, it offers some of the joy of original creation without much of the travail. There is pleasure in it whenever you are satisfied that, in your own eyes at least, your version is more nearly right than anyone else's, and your ingenious devices in at least a respectable ratio to your many inevitable frustrations and failures. Occasionally it can lead to praise and even to a little money. And it is admirably adapted to the busy life of the academic year, when all too often we simply cannot in decency set aside much consecutive time for those enterprises that require it. With translation, on the other hand, if you get a few hours on it one day and then no more for perhaps several weeks or a month or more, you can usually still pick it up whenever you do have time almost exactly where, and as, you left off. That, in fact, is how I have worked on much of the translation—probably most of it, indeed—that I have done.

I suppose most of us get into translation in about the same way. We take a look at someone else's translation of a work we love and say, preferably to ourselves: "Good Lord, I think *I* could do better than that!" It was that and nepotism that got me started, and Montaigne.[1]

Donald Frame is best known for his translations of the complete works of Montaigne. He has also translated works by Voltaire, Prévost, and Molière. His translation of François Rabelais's oeuvre is near completion.

1. Since my doctoral dissertation concerned Montaigne, my late aunt Louise R. Loomis suggested my name to prepare a Classics Club edition of Montaigne's *Selected Essays,* which led to this being my first published translation (1943).

For me percentages figure in translation, or at least estimates of relative feasibility. A prospective translator can look at a text and make an estimate of its maximum yield in his language: say 20 percent or 50, or even 80 percent. (If it's 100 percent or even close to that, it may not be challenging or at all interesting and may be one of the texts best left to the machines.) But if he thinks he can do a 15 percent job where 20 percent is the maximum, a 40 percent job where tops would be 50, or 70 percent where it is 80, it may well be worth trying—especially if the best available other version seems to give much less of a yield. Let me illustrate what I mean by these percentages, using some poetry to show the problems more clearly. First example—Verlaine:

Les sanglots longs
Des violons
De l'automne
Blessent mon coeur
D'une langueur
Monotone.

You can of course render the *meaning* of the French easily enough:

The long sobs
Of the violins
Of autumn
Wound my heart
With a monotonous
Languor.

But when you do, what happens to the sound: the soft nasals (*ang, ong*), liquids (*l, r*), mute *e*'s, long languid syllables? And for that matter to the rhythm, muted but firm? All gone, no? And with them, I should say, a good 80 percent of the beauty of the original;

Parenthetical references to Montaigne are to book and chapter, with page references to the Villey-Saulnier edition (VS) for the French and to my translation of *Complete Works* and *Complete Essays* (same pagination for both), noted as S, for Stanford University Press. Molière quotations are from my translation *The Misanthrope and Other Plays* (1968); quotations from Voltaire are from my translation *Candide, Zadig, and Selected Stories* (1961); and those from Prévost are from my translation *Manon Lescaut* (1961, 1983), all published by New American Library.

for the sense is surely unremarkable. Maximum yield, about 20
percent or less.
  Another example—Racine:

  La fille de Minos et de Pasiphaë.

  For beauty of cadence and sound, some critics rate this line
very high, among the loveliest in the language. Yet it is also brimful
of content, for here for the first time, after some 35 lines, Racine
has someone (appropriately, her beloved and future victim Hip-
polyte) allude to the ominous figure, and still more ominous background, of the heroine, Phèdre. The name Minos recalls not only
that king, her father, but also her monstrous half-brother, the Min-
otaur; that of Pasiphaë (her mother and its mother), the revolting
lust for the bull that Venus inflicted on the poor queen of Crete,
and hence the tainted blood that flows in Phèdre's veins; and they
recall this politely, decorously, with the power of a muffled explo-
sion. If you render this, as I think you must, "Daughter of Minos
and Pasiphaë," for all the beauty of sound you lose, I think you still
keep around 40 percent or so of the original.
  A third and last example—Hugo:

  Un frais parfum sortait des touffes d'asphodèle,
  Les souffles de la nuit flottaient sur Galgala.

  Here, as in the Verlaine example, the sounds are obviously par-
amount: mainly the *f*'s and soft *s*'s, as well as the *l*'s and *r*'s, all
contributing even more than the meaning to the sense of soft
breeze and perfumed hush. This looks like a low-yield bit, perhaps
another one good for 20 percent or less, and I think this is true of
the second line: certainly anything like the literal "the breaths of
night floated over Galgala" seems to me to fall in that range. But
note the hazards, and in this case the long-shot winners of translation. Take the first line quite literally: "A fresh perfume issued from
the tufts of asphodel." The rhythm is a bit shot, but the sounds are
almost the same—more so still if you sacrificed meaning a bit and
rendered *sortait* by "sifted," or went further yet and made the line
"A fresh perfume suffused the tufts of asphodel." Anyway, surpris-
ingly, and more by good luck than by skill, I would say you can get
around 50 or 60 percent.

My experience is limited to one language, French, probably one of the easiest to put into English because French and English share a vast common stock of Latin-derived syntax and vocabulary, and the like. Translation from French into English presents, from what I have observed, relatively few special problems. To be sure, there are some. We are helpless anywhere that the *tu-vous* distinction is important. Tenses can offer insuperable difficulties. In Camus's *L'Etranger,* for example, it must be frustrating to know from the very first sentence, "Aujourd'hui maman est morte," that you haven't a prayer of conveying the confusion of past and present, the dislocation of time, that Camus achieves simply by using the *passé composé* (or *indéfini*), instead of the *passé simple* (or *défini*) as the tense for simple past narrative. A frequent problem, though of course not confined to French and English, is in formulas of politeness—and of impoliteness, such as the oaths in Molière and elsewhere. These rarely correspond exactly between two languages—or different moments in one language: you must usually overdo or underdo. Moreover, they tend to date rather rapidly; but if you try to match the dating you may wind up with a "Zounds and Gadzooks" translation. One extreme example of a formula problem: how do you *translate* literally "Veuillez agréer, cher Monsieur, l'expression de mes sentiments distingués?" "Be so kind as to look with favor, dear Sir, on the expression of my distinguished sentiments?" Or, rendering the meaning, as I suppose we must (I haven't had to—yet), "Yours sincerely," or "Yours truly"? One way lies madness, the other at best inadequacy. How should you render "Monsieur le Baron"? "His (or Your) Lordship the Baron," or simply "Baron"? This, I think, depends on the context and the feel, like so much else in translation; either one may be right in the right place. But then what of "Monsieur l'abbé" or "Monsieur le prieur," "(The) Abbot (or Prior)" or "(the) Reverend Abbot (or Prior)"? Or simply "Abbot"? And what if, as *does* happen, the abbot in question is very much a monsieur but not conspicuously reverend? I suspect you had best keep it as "Monsieur l'abbé." One curious similar case: In *Candide,* how should you translate the "mademoiselle" in "Mademoiselle Cunégonde"? "Miss"? "Fräulein"? (After all, she *is* German.) Hardly, I think. You keep it in French. But if so, why? In this case, on what principle?

The range of what I have translated is not great: all of it French, from periods extending from the sixteenth century (my special field: all Montaigne and Rabelais) through the seventeenth

(Molière, fourteen comedies) to the eighteenth (Prévost's *Manon Lescaut* and sixteen tales by Voltaire). And all I have done so far, unless I have missed the boat very badly, is relatively high yield, in a range perhaps of 50 to 80 percent. A major question with all such authors as these, of earlier times, is that of tone, under which I would subsume that of language, more of which later. How natural, how stylized, should each translation be? The answer must of course depend on the individual author and work.

I will start with three of the four authors I have rendered, to try to illustrate my general statement with specific examples. For *Manon Lescaut* the main problem is one of tone and balance. This is the one brief masterpiece of a very prolific writer, Abbé Antoine-François Prévost (1697–1763), who also emitted vast quantities of dreadful corn, in style as well as substance. However, he took pride, and rightly, in the simplicity of this one work, as we see from this third-person account in a prefatory bit:

> Je ne dis rien du style de cet ouvrage. Il n'y a ni jargon, ni affectation, ni réflexions sophistiques; c'est la Nature même qui écrit. Qu'un auteur empesé et fardé paraît pitoyable en comparaison! Celui-ci ne court point après l'esprit, ou plutôt après ce qu'on appelle ainsi. Ce n'est point un style laconiquement constipé, mais un style coulant, plein et expressif. Ce n'est partout que peintures et sentiments, mais des peintures vraies et des sentiments naturels.

> I say nothing about the style of this work. There is neither jargon, nor affectation, nor sophistic reflections; it is Nature herself writing. How pitiful a starched and rouged author appears in comparison! This one does not go chasing after wit, or rather after that which is so called. This is not a laconically constipated style, but a flowing, full, and expressive one. This offers nothing save portraits and feelings, but they are true portraits and natural feelings. (P. cv)

This statement, however self-serving, is a pretty good guide, and in the main, *Manon Lescaut* speaks quite directly to the modern reader. However, it often has a period flavor of sentimentality, politeness, and either corrupt innocence or innocent corruption, which is not unique in eighteenth-century France but is not our own. It reflects an author and time for whom good manners were a morality in themselves much as honesty is for many today. The translator must try to keep this balance and blend of tones that he finds in the French. I found four English versions to reckon with. Tancock, in Penguin, has some flair but wastes much of it by making Prévost (or Des Grieux, his hero-narrator throughout) sound too contemporary. The "standard" translation by D. C. Moylan, and even more the newer one by John Danton, get more of the flavor but too often miss the meaning. For example, when Des Grieux is trying to think how to hide from Manon his loss of some money lest he lose her, he says at one point, "Le Ciel me donna une idée". And I feel sure he means just that: the idea came from heaven, which surely must favor lovers in distress (p. 58). Moylan and Tancock let this go simply as "an idea came to me" or the like. Later Des Grieux explains that when young Monsieur de T helped him free Manon from the hôpital, he did so partly in the hope of sharing Manon's favors (p. 98). Danton translates this hope (*l'espérance*) as "the promise," which would seem to mean a promise from Des Grieux. Now Des Grieux's moral code is all his own— and Prévost's, but such a promise from him would be unthinkable.

The best of the four is that of Helen Waddell, who is faithful and seeks, with considerable success, to follow the rhythm of the original. (I differ slightly on her choice of editions—that of 1731 rather than that of 1753—but I understand and respect it.) At all events, even she nods sometimes, as in this passage (in which the 1731 and 1753 texts are identical) from the letter Manon left for Des Grieux when she abandoned him in favor of the wealthy Monsieur de G.M.: "Crois-tu qu'on puisse être bien tendre, lorsqu'on manque de pain? La faim me causerait quelque méprise fatale; je rendrais quelque jour le dernier soupir, en croyant en pousser un d'amour." This I take to mean: "Do you think one can be very tender when one has no bread? Hunger would lead me into some fatal mistake: some day I should give my last sigh and think it was for love" (p. 71). Helen Waddell renders it thus: "Do you think one can make love when one has nothing to eat? Hunger would cheat me to death; some day I should give my last sigh and think it was for love." The "cheat me to death" bothers me a little here, and the "make love" bothers me more than a little. To be sure, this is exactly what Manon *means* by "be very tender"; but it is emphatically *not* what she would say.

I've translated fourteen comedies by Molière (nine prose, five verse), after itching for many years to try it, the more so since in our Columbia College books course my students and I had suffered for years from really bad Molière translations, notably the old

76   DONALD FRAME

"standard" one in Modern Library by Van Laun, who had a genuine talent for dullness. (Most of my comments will bear on the verse plays.) Then suddenly in the 1950s there appeared some good Molière in English by two able translators. First, in 1950, Morris Bishop published a fine *Malade imaginaire (The Would-Be Invalid)*, in Crofts Classics, with a truly inspired rendition of the macaronic examination-reception of Argan as a doctor of medicine, more of which later; and several years afterward another eight, including most of Molière's finest, in Modern Library. Meanwhile, in 1955, Richard Wilbur gave us his *Misanthrope*, in rhymed verse as in the French; and with those ten versions (that and Bishop's nine) I thought we had our English Molière for some time; perhaps we do. It seemed to me that Wilbur's one in rhymed verse had quite surpassed Bishop's nine in the unrhymed; yet Wilbur's *Misanthrope*, though charming and elegant, seemed at times not to give enough sense of what the man said. I didn't want to try any Molière unless I found I would do a *Misanthrope* quite different from Wilbur's but of comparable quality. When I tried it, I found to my surprise that my version would be very different from his, as I tried to keep a share of his grace and still stay closer to the original. The main problem I found (that I am aware of) was that of condensing Molière's Alexandrines down from their twelve syllables to the ten-syllable pentameter that seems to be the only English meter natural enough to use. The differences in length from language to language seemed to even out: translating often makes a text longer, but English is normally more concise than French. As a rule something had to be cut: usually either a key word or one of the many (usually initial) *et, mais,* or *donc* that abound in Molière and seem less indispensable. Cut a key word, and the sense of the whole line suffers; cut an initial conjunction or adverb, and the sense is usually less damaged, but the lines come out sententious and a bit epigrammatic, more like run-of-the-mill Alexander Pope than like Molière, and the fluidity and movement of the verse is often lost. This is a typical translator's problem, where he must prefer the lesser of two evils. I naturally prefer to retain the key words, but since seeing the problem, I have tried to keep a balance.

    Of course the big problem in translating Molière's—or any other—verse plays is double: are we to put them into verse or prose? And if verse, into rhymed or unrhymed verse? Of course they are rhymed in French, but that was then easily their dominant tradition and is still a live one, whereas for sustained verse, English has usually preferred the unrhymed (Shakespeare, Milton, et al.). I think the answers are different for each poet: how important is verse, and rhymed verse, to his work? If we keep both verse and rhyme, how much must we sacrifice for that? Richard Wilbur has made the case well for rhymed verse for Molière and has backed his theory with practice. I am puzzled that Morris Bishop, a connoisseur of Molière and superb comic poet (*Spilt Milk,* "Ozymandias Revisited"), did not put him into rhyme. Perhaps he did not want to devote that much time and energy to translation. Despite the quality of his versions, I find them not nearly as good as Wilbur's, and I think they gain little by giving up the rhyme. An earlier translator who put the verse plays quite well into unrhymed verse, Curtis Hidden Page, noted that it was often hard to avoid rhyme; clearly it is harder to write acceptable unrhymed verse than rhymed. In short, I favor rhymed verse for Molière's rhymed verse and have used it there.

Here let me fall back on a few illustrations from *The Misanthrope* to show how I differ from Wilbur, some of the problems this has posed, and how I have tried to solve them. I have tried in these to show differences, not just my own supposed superiority, but I may well have chosen in the hope of showing both. I present about twenty lines, a few at a time, in three forms each: Molière's French, Wilbur's English, and my English.

In act 1, scene 1 (lines 118–22), Alceste, the champion of candor, has rebuked his friend Philinte for insincere politeness and said that to him all men are odious. Does your hate extend to all, Philinte asks, or are some exempt? Alceste replies:

Molière   Non, elle est générale, et je hais tous les hommes,
          Les uns parce qu'ils sont méchants et malfaisants,
          Et les autres pour être aux méchants complaisants,
          Et n'avoir pas pour eux ces haines vigoureuses
          Que doit donner le vice aux âmes vertueuses.

Wilbur   No, I include all men in one dim view:
          Some men I hate for being rogues; the others
          I hate because they treat the rogues like brothers,
          And lacking a virtuous scorn for what is vile,
          Receive the villain with a complaisant smile.

Frame   No, it is general; I hate all men;
          For some are wholly bad in thought and deed;

The others, seeing this, take little heed;
For they are too indulgent and too nice
To share the hate that virtue has for vice.

Here is part of Philinte's reply twenty-odd lines later:

Molière   Mon Dieu, des moeurs du temps mettons-nous moins en
              peine,
           Et faisons un peu grâce à la nature humaine;
           Ne l'examinons point dans la grande rigueur,
           Et voyons ses défauts avec quelque douceur.

Wilbur   This world requires a pliant rectitude;
           Too stern a virtue makes one stiff and rude.
           Good sense views all extremes with detestation,
           And bids us to be noble in moderation.

Frame   In this world virtue needs more tact than rigor;
           Wisdom may be excessive in its vigor;
           Perfected reason flees extremity;
           Bids us be wise, but with sobriety.

One last sample from *The Misanthrope*. In act 1, scene 2, the fatuous Oronte insists on reading to Alceste the inane sonnet he has composed. After holding back at length with little more than hints, Alceste finally tells him what he thinks of it and how much he prefers the crude candor of such an old song as this:

Molière   Si le roi m'avait donné
           Paris, sa grand' ville
           Et qu'il me fallût quitter
           L'amour de ma mie,
           Je dirais au roi Henri
           Reprenez votre Paris,
           J'aime mieux ma mie, au gué,
           J'aime mieux ma mie.

Wilbur   If the King had given me for my own
           Paris, his citadel,
           And I for that must leave alone
           Her whom I love so well,
           I'd say then to the Crown
           Take back your glittering town,

> My darling is more fair, I swear,
> My darling is more fair.

Frame   If the King had given me
> Great Paris for my own,
> And had said the price must be
> To leave my love alone,
> I would tell the king Henri,
> Just take back your great Paris,
> I prefer my love, heigh ho,
> I prefer my love.

I hope these samples convey some idea of what I've tried to do with Molière, some of the problems I've had, and some of the characteristic differences between Wilbur's version and mine. If I had a chance (or ever do in future) to put out a revision of mine, I would reduce the number of "cheap" rhymes (not peculiar to mine, by the way), as I now see them: overly easy ones, such as Latinate derivatives in -ate, -ize, -ion, -ity, and the like, which weary me when I see a verse translation of mine (the *Tartuffe*, to be specific) performed; I used so many just because I was working in a hurry.

I've spent this long on problems of verse for several reasons: first, these are the only pieces of sustained verse I have translated; second, Wilbur has rendered only four plays of Molière, all in verse; third, the only one of his translated plays in print when I started doing mine was his *Misanthrope;* and fourth, anyway, I think that play best shows our differences and priorities.

One problem he has not confronted, in Molière at least, is that of dialect or patois, for in Molière's verse plays there is none, since any plebeian or rustic characters are very minor. This is not the case with some characters in prose plays, such as *Don Juan* and *The Doctor in Spite of Himself,* the two where I have run afoul of it. The full chapter on patois that it probably deserves must here be summed up in this sentence: I doubt that it can ever be satisfactorily translated for a geographically varied audience. Put Molière's Ile-de-France patois into Yorkshire, say, and you may ring a bell with an Englishman but will merely confuse an American; the converse is true if you use Kentucky hillbilly. I suspect that for each Anglophone country of some magnitude—Australia, Canada, New Zealand, South Africa in its Anglophone aspect, perhaps even India—there is at least one leading candidate, probably several, for a solution, and subject to change in time as well. Molière's dialect

French put in the mouths of his country bumpkins, the patois of the Ile-de-France countryside surrounding Paris, abounds in solecisms such as *j'avons*, mispronunciations (by Paris standards at least) such as *bian* for *bien*, *naye* for *noye* (then pronounced *nweye*), *stapandant* for *cependant;* rustic near-oaths and exclamations such as *ma fi, testiguenne, jerniquenne, parquieene, mon quieu*, and the like. I have tried for what seemed to me comparable effects with such forms as "drownded," "land's sakes," "doggone it," "tarnation," "listen here," "jeepers," and so on. Granted, I am hardly addicted to dialect stories and literature. I have seen no other attempts that I like any better for these plays, but I still feel as I did when I translated them: that of all fourteen, *Don Juan* was the one that most effectively defied adequate English translation, and I am much less than ecstatic over my own end product in these two plays.

Voltaire seemed to me to present rather few problems, at least in the sixteen tales I translated. I have mentioned those of his nobiliary and other titles—"Monsieur le baron," "Monsieur l'abbé," and the like—but of course these are in no way peculiar to him. A minor one was the names of the couple in *Zadig* called "L'Envieux" and "La Femme de l'Envieux," and the larger one of the hero of *L'Ingénu*. The last named (to start with him) has been rendered as "The Huron," "the child of nature," and a number of things which he may or may not be (after all, a Huron he is not, except by a sort of adoption); nothing in English is both accurate and crisp, as the French is. I decided to call him simply "Ingenuous." The reader soon gets used to it, I think. Our language abounds in analogous nicknames such as Red, Lefty, Slim, Curly, and some of Voltaire's crispness is retained. I did the same thing with L'Envieux (Envious), but his wife gave me trouble. "The wife of Envious" seems most unnatural, "Envious's wife" cacophonous, "Madame Envious" awkwardly bilingual. The best solution I could find was simply "Mrs. Envious."

I think the main point in translating Voltaire is to avoid explaining his jokes and wit by overexplicit translation, or if I may quote myself on this, "to keep out of his way," since "in my opinion he speaks excellent English." Here are two problems, however, that concern fidelity. Voltaire loves to move in past narratives from the simple past (*passé simple* or *passé défini*) into the historical present—sometimes for only two verbs or even for only one—and then back again. Here is an example from *Candide*, chapter 7:

La vieille reparut bientôt; elle soutenait avec peine une femme trem-
blante . . . Otez ce voile, dit la vieille à Candide. Le jeune homme
approche; il lève le voile . . . il croit voir Mlle Cunégonde, il la voyait
en effet, c'était elle-même. La force lui manque, il ne peut proférer
une parole, il tombe à ses pieds. Cunégonde tombe sur le canapé.

The old woman soon reappeared; she was supporting with difficulty
a trembling woman . . . Remove that veil, said (or, says) the old
woman to Candide. The young man approaches, he lifts the veil . . .
He thinks he sees Mlle Cunégonde, he did indeed see her, it was she
herself. His strength fails him, he cannot utter a word, he falls at her
feet. Cunégonde falls on the sofa. [No fool she.]

If we follow suit in English in this way, is the effect the same?
I think not quite; a little more surprising. But I think we come
closer to the effect of the French if we do follow Voltaire's tense
changes than if, with most translators, we ignore them entirely and
leave everything in the simple past. I compromised, however, since
the translator must mediate as well as render (but beware of the
proverbial *traduttore-traditore,* "translator-traitor"): I moved into
the present only when Voltaire stays there for at least two verbs in
a row or in rapid succession. This is a characteristic *type* of problem
for the translator.

My second problem (of the two I announced a while back) is
one of those caused by the simplest kind of statement. I have great
respect for Richard Aldington's translation of *Candide,* which for
years seemed to be the standard one and perhaps still is. For many
years, however, I had thought his was a poor translation because
of one word on the very first page. Of the heroine's father, the
Baron of Thunder-ten-Tronckh, Voltaire writes that his dogs
served as hounds, his grooms as huntsmen, and so on, and adds:
"Ils l'appelaient tous Monseigneur, et ils riaient quand il faisait des
contes." Aldington renders this thus: "They all called him My
Lord, and laughed heartily at his stories." This is crisp, to be sure,
but the gratuitous "heartily" seemed appalling in a version of Voltaire, who rarely uses an unnecessary word. But why the "heartily"?
From translating it myself I have guessed a possible reason. To me
at least the French makes it quite clear that they were laughing *with*
him (however obsequiously), not *at* him because his stories were
duds. And somehow the straight English version, "They laughed
when he told stories," seems in contrast a bit ambiguous. Now a
translation of Voltaire must not be ambiguous unless when he is

purposefully so. I rendered this, "They laughed at the stories he told," which errs by making explicit a causal relationship that Voltaire leaves to the reader. If I ever have another chance at it, I plan to say "And when he told stories, they laughed."

An added "heartily" is of course a minor flaw. One habit of some translators really bewilders me: their refusal to translate things they know their author is saying. (The three hundred–page Dell Voltaire, edited by Edmund Fuller: Friar Giroflée changed from a monk into a guardsman, and the monastery where he wanted to beat his head out every night into a barracks; no pejorative reference is left in the story to any religious order. Another category: the W. F. Smith version of Rabelais, that leaves many coarse chapters in French; and the "fig leaf" Ives translation of Montaigne, which also leaves in French all obscene passages, and with them one of Montaigne's longest and richest chapters, 3:5, "On Some Verses of Virgil." This at least is not misleading; though you sometimes get the bizarre impression that Montaigne wrote in French, at least when he wanted to be very naughty. These I find more understandable than the puzzling phenomenon of the Dell volume.)

Does this mean that I see no value at all in that volume? Not at all; in fact I am indebted to it for a good solution to one problem that had baffled others before me. In *Zadig,* for one brief early moment the hero enjoys the success and happiness he deserves. Recently imprisoned for some supposedly seditious verses, he has been freed once a parrot finds and returns the other half of the tablet inscribed with those verses, which shows their innocence. Zadig of course seeks out and thanks the parrot, ending by musing aloud to the bird: "un bonheur si étrange sera peut-être bientôt évanoui." The parrot replies, "oui." No earlier translator had managed to convey this prophetic psittacism. I forget the exact rendering in the Dell, but I borrowed it in this form: "So strange a happiness perhaps will vanish soon." The parrot answered "Soon."

This leads me to another digression. I strongly favor regarding translation, like scholarship, as a cumulative undertaking, and therefore borrowing—or stealing—whenever you see that your own best solution to a problem is clearly inferior to someone else's. There are exceptions, of course: versions so unmistakably marked with the translator's stamp that you cannot do this, such as Morris Bishop's marvelous chorus late in *The Imaginary Invalid:* "Give'e-mam enemam, / N'enemam purgemam; / N'eneman bleedemam purgemam againemam"—one of the rare cases where I believe a translator has improved on the original. But apart from such near-miracles, I would put the question thus: Why shouldn't translation be like scholarship in this respect, that X is a bad scholar if his findings ignore or neglect the valuable earlier ones of scholar Y? My reasons are obvious, I think: translations are legion and proliferating; most are mediocre, many very poor; but to check them carefully takes much time and some expertise. This being so, it is inhumane, to put it mildly, to bring out a translation which even you, as translator, *know* is inferior to another in important points. (Of course there are exceptional situations; for example, in rhyming couplets you must often sacrifice something in one line for the sake of its mate and the couplet.) To this shameless confession about borrowing I hasten to add two points:

1. Unless you believe you can markedly improve on all existing translations, and do that without anthologizing (combining everyone else's best parts), I don't think you should translate for publication. There are more honest ways to spend time and seek recognition, including, as Swift might say, teaching, stealing, public service, arson, hijacking, scholarship, and pimping. But how to be sure the improvement you have made is marked? That is often very hard indeed to say.

2. If you accept this notion that translation should be cumulative, you must of course be ready to be pillaged yourself by any new translator who generally likes your work but thinks he can improve on parts of it.

Let me now turn for a short while to Rabelais and then return in conclusion to Montaigne.

Clearly Rabelais offers more problems than anyone I have attempted, and I may live to repent this venture. Apparently, all four others that I have translated at least wrote to be understood; much of the time Rabelais obviously writes to mystify. They use language mainly to convey meaning; he, often for the sound and for the sheer delight of playing with that wonderful new toy, words—for so they must have seemed in the early light of the age of printing. (Their power: Hugo's "Ceci tuera cela.") All the others (despite the apparent difficulty of Montaigne's spelling) wrote in a French not far removed from today's. Rabelais's, though only fifty years before Montaigne, is remote indeed; for a sense of it, imagine Joyce writing in the English of Chaucer or perhaps of Milton. In writing about Rabelais in 1977, I questioned whether he was adequately translatable into English, as I think Montaigne is, and I found available English versions so faulty that I used my own instead. However, although only one of these is still in print, five have been published since Rabelais's day. I reviewed four of the five cursorily back in 1951 apropos of John Cowper Powys's *Rabelais,* which combines a brief study of the man and the book with a translation of about a quarter of the text and a statement of the needs of the translator. Of this last in particular I then wrote:

> His ideas on translating Rabelais are excellent. He finds Urquhart guilty of inflating (and depreciating) Rabelais's "humor of character" into "humor of comical extravagance" by piling on his own details, and supports this charge with an apt illustration. W. F. Smith's version, quite scholarly and accurate but avoiding obscenities and thus leaving some chapters in French, he rightly labels "too stately, courtly, and refined." He thinks Samuel Putnam's modernization brilliant but often dangerously anachronistic. He does not know the translation of Jacques Leclercq, who mars his brilliant virtuosity when he out-Urquharts Urquhart in his readiness to improve—and enlarge—on the original. Powys's aim is fidelity without sacrifice of vigor and freshness: as good an aim as can be imagined.
>
> The ideal translator of Rabelais should combine, among other qualities, the imagination, daring, and gusto of the gifted creative writer with the learned humility of the good scholar. Mr. Powys has all the requisite qualities except, apparently, an unerring knowledge of Rabelais's French. He sometimes misses the sense, sometimes is unnecessarily verbose. All in all, however, his translation of about one-fourth of Rabelais seems to me the best we have in English.

I have said nothing yet about the one available translation, by J. M. Cohen for Penguin, since it was published in 1955, after I had written that review. I consider it not bad, but not really good either. It has neither the scholarly fidelity of that of Smith (1893), nor the sprightly resourcefulness of the old Urquhart–Le Motteux. Specifically, Cohen is uneven in rendering Rabelais's proper names, and at times sadly mistaken when a basic knowledge of sixteenth-century French is essential. Let me illustrate briefly. French proper names in Rabelais usually state or suggest (sometimes by comic antiphrasis) the character's nature, thus calling for direct translation or approximation. Thus "Dungby" is all right for *Merdaille,* "Swashbuckler" correct for *Spadassin.* Cohen's treatment of names of other originals, however, is often less felicitous. That of the one sane member of Picrochole's council of war in *Gargantua* (1:33, p. 112), *Echephron* ("having mind or sense"), is twice mistreated on that one page in ways having neither mind nor sense, *Ecephron* and *Eciphron,* which suggest that for Cohen "Graecum est; non legitur." One of the authorities whom Panurge consults in book 3 about whether or not to marry, the Pyrrhonian philosopher whose answer to all questions is in effect "Yes, or No, or either, or neither, or both," is called *Trouillogan,* which suggests no apparent meaning. Yet Cohen calls him "Wordspinner"—a name not misleading but wholly gratuitous. And whereas Rabelais names that comic but repulsive fanatic the bishop of Papimania *Homenaz,* Cohen calls him "Greatclod," which may well be appropriate but is not the point. In the strongly Gallican mood of 1551 in France, with the Council of Trent rigged by the pro-Italians, *Homenaz,* which equals *Homme-Nez* ("Man-Nose" or "Nose-Man"), clearly designates the archenemy of King Henry II and of France at that time, Pope Julius III, renowned for his prodigious proboscis.

Cohen's greatest weakness, however, is his ignorance of sixteenth-century French, which in one critical spot leads him to render Rabelais's text by its exact opposite. After building up an apparent case for a silenic hidden meaning in *Gargantua,* Rabelais's discourse goes into a zigzag: do you believe there is any such meaning in Homer? If you do, implicitly, you're a fool. If you don't, why don't you do as much with this book of mine? (Up to here, his aim is unclear: does "do as much" mean "to read in" or "to regard reading in as folly"?) But then he adds, "combien que, les dictans, n'y pensasse en plus que vous, qui par adventure beviez comme moy." The *combien que* ("although"; modern French *bien que*) makes it fully clear that he is inviting us *to read in,* "although as I wrote I had no such idea in my head, any more than did you, who were perhaps drinking as I was." Cohen, however, by translating *combien que* (p. 39) by its opposite, *seeing that,* renders the first part of the sentence as an invitation *not to read in,* which nullifies Rabelais's entire game of mystification with the reader here. Nor is this the only such instance, merely the worst.

Two characteristics make Rabelais difficult, if not impossible, to translate adequately: this love of mystification, of riddles and enigmas, and what has been aptly called his lexicographical intoxication (again the affinities with Joyce are evident). Rabelais is indeed drunk with words. Now of course we have all been taught, it

sometimes seems from the cradle, that in writing, economy is one
of the greatest virtues, perhaps *the* greatest. And this is not just
since Hemingway made such a fetish of it; in seventeenth- and
eighteenth-century France it was exemplified by such giants as Pascal, La Rochefoucauld, Voltaire, and many others. Pascal apolo-
gized for making one of his *Provincial Letters* so long, saying he had
lacked the time to make it shorter. Nor, after all, was the epigram,
or laconic speech, unknown to the ancient Greeks and Romans—
no doubt among many others. Why use ten words, we say, if three
will do? Rabelais loves to turn the question around and ask in effect: why limit ourselves to ten words when there are hundreds,
nay thousands, of beauties just waiting to be used? Clearly he had
a good knowledge of several rich languages: French and Latin of
course, Greek, some Hebrew—and, apparently, at least a smatter-
ing of several others as well as of many dialects or patois. Thus he
had a prodigious vocabulary and delighted in using it. His book
abounds in lists, often numbering in the hundreds, of nouns, attri-
butes, proper names, verbs, and the like, usually so long that they
are set off typographically as such. A friend of mine undertook not
long ago a study of Rabelais's terms for the verb "to copulate" and
found, as I recall, 36 in all, of which 14, I think it was, were of
Rabelais's own invention—and mind you, obscene as he certainly
is, Rabelais is not in the least pornographic, far less so than almost
any contemporary novelist. The love of play in Rabelais extends far
beyond the vocabulary but includes it, as in that cousin of the
spoonerism that the French then called *équivocquer,* as when in *Pan-
tagruel* (2:21, Pl. 262) Panurge tells the Parisian lady he is after,
"équivocquez sur *A Beaumont le Vicomte.*" Or in comparable phenomena such as *la coupe testée* or *la coupe gorgée* (for *la gorge coupée*
or *la tête coupée*). An inversion of ideas or rather nouns with non-
sense effect is *je tuerais un peigne pour un mercier,* or roughly "I
would kill a comb for (in order to steal) a haberdasher"; today it
would be a drugstore clerk, at least in American English. All these
might be included in the realm of apparent *lapsus linguae* or slips
of the tongue, but even if so, that makes it no easier to translate
them. I have thought of a few of these and of other phenomena
that strike me as similar and that I think Rabelais might have enjoyed—mangled proverbs or sayings such as "a watched clock
never boils," "he knows which side his bed is buttered on," where
I still "wow" myself with the comic incongruity, and I have imagined a few obscene *équivocques* (my noun here from *équivocquer*)

which I can produce on demand. But I suspect I have much more to find in this area, where I have thought from the first I would have the most trouble, for I have never before tackled an author with such a wild, often manic, surrealistic imagination.

Let me now turn to Montaigne in conclusion, as the author I know much the best and have translated completely (and in parts often, over many years). To begin, let me raise about him the question of the period of English to use if one can in translating him. Supposing the translator controlled an earlier English well enough to translate into it, which should it be? Always a likely candidate, of course, is that of the author's lifetime, in this case the English of the 1580s and 1590s. That's what we have in Florio, and his translation deservedly had the impact of the first one and became a monument in our literature. Yet the strengths and weaknesses of that English correspond only poorly, as the Florio shows, with that of Montaigne: Florio is too flowery, too euphuistic, too decorative, not "down-to-earth" enough; the metaphor is too rarely the very expression and embodiment of the thought or idea. Should we then move on in time and use the English of Sir Thomas Browne, or later of Laurence Sterne? Or still later of Emerson? All are eminent admirers of Montaigne with some stylistic debt to him. But they lead us one, two, three centuries away from him; would four be much worse? I think not. Again, I think the big question here is one of tone: to what extent an author seems to speak to us directly today. (Rabelais, for example, cultivates archaism as one of his games with his reader. Montaigne does not, and while his French is by no means modern in spelling and not wholly so in vocabulary and syntax, most of the difference in these respects is simply a matter of time. What is his own we must seek to reproduce as best we can in whatever English we use: what I like to call his shagginess, his determination to make a reluctant language accept the accurate and vivid metaphors by which he makes the abstract concrete.) To any ready reader of sixteenth-century French, Montaigne—much like Villon a century earlier in this respect— seems to speak very directly and in no archaic accents. In all such cases I think we are justified in using an English that is fully and intelligibly contemporary but not merely so, that has stood the test of time for a while and seems likely to stand it for a while longer.

Does this mean that an anachronism is never justified? Perhaps hardly ever, as Gilbert and Sullivan might say, but certainly not

never. In Montaigne's chapter "Of Vanity" (3:9), speaking of men
nearing death and craving sympathy for this, he writes: "J'en ay
veu prendre la chevre" (literally, "take the goat") when they failed
to receive it. When I first translated this passage, I of course wanted
to render it "I have seen it get some men's goat" (for that is just
what it means). But I cowed myself with doctrinaire sophistry and
instead wrote meekly: "I have seen some men get angry." Soon
after, another translator put this as I should have done from the
first. As soon as I saw it in print I knew he was right, and luckily I
have had the chance to change mine since (p. S748). Vigor and
picturesqueness must be held on to tooth and nail in Montaigne.
There is a comparable problem in "Presumption" (2:17), where
Montaigne, speaking of the know-it-alls who "perch on the epicy-
cle of Mercury," says "ils m'arrachent les dents." Here the literal
"they yank out my teeth" is theoretically wrong, since this figurative use is more alien to English usage than to French. Should we
then settle for "they give me a pain," "they get on my nerves," or
the like? I think not; so here I chose, rightly I think, the vivid,
vigorous "yank out my teeth" (as others do not) because here the
context seems to make the figurative meaning, even in English,
promptly and abundantly clear. In another context I might have
had to settle for clarity at the expense of vigor.

A dull and rather persistent problem is Montaigne's fondness
for long strings of phrases with present or perfect participles, as
here in his chapter "Of Sadness" (1:2, 7): "But the story goes that
Psammenitus, king of Egypt, after his defeat and capture by Cam-
byses, king of Persia, seeing his daughter pass before him as a prisoner, dressed as a servant and on her way to draw water, all his
friends around him weeping and lamenting, he himself neither
moved nor spoke a word, his eyes fixed on the ground. And further, seeing his son presently being led to his death, he held himself
to this same demeanor. But having seen one of his friends led
among the captives, he began to beat his head and manifest extreme grief."

I think that modern speech habits demand that we break these
up sometimes, and I have done so even in translating this passage,
as page 7 of my translation will show. However, I think there is a
connection (not very clear here) between this habit and the
suppression of connectives (asyndeton) that Erich Auerbach, in
Mimesis, brought out so well in "Repentance" (3:2) and in Montaigne in general; that it relates to Montaigne's apparent reluctance

to claim omniscience about causal or concessive relationships: even as he leaves it to us to supply an implicit (but not furnished) "and," "for," or "but," which is roughly Auerbach's point, so here he lets us choose between a temporal, causal, or concessive use of the participle.

A kindred problem, because in my opinion insoluble, is Montaigne's occasional nonstop sentences (or sort of sentences), such as those on the qualities of Alexander the Great (2:36, 571–72) and the still longer one (3–5, 649–50) on the difficulty of chastity for women and the unfairness of men's demands and expectations of them in this respect. Unless I am quite blind, these are not at all Proustian types of nonstoppers, delicately organized chambered nautiluses of prose; rather they are like the phrase about Britain's empire, absentminded agglomerations. I think you must keep them as best you can—they are part of Montaigne. But I hope it is common sense, not cowardice, that suggests some occasional reminder to the puzzled reader of where he is.

With Montaigne we must constantly remember that his style, as he tells us himself (3:5, 667), is part of his self-portrait; we smooth it out at our peril. Let me illustrate. J. M. Cohen, a fair-to-middling translator of Rabelais and Cervantes, in his Penguin volume of selected essays of Montaigne, has given a most curious version of a great passage in the essays which is almost their conclusion (3:13, 857): "C'est une absolue perfection, et comme divine, de savoir jouir loyalement de son estre," which I think can, and should, be taken quite directly: "It is an absolute perfection and virtually divine to know how to enjoy our being rightfully." To me the only problem here is how to translate the rich *loyalement*. It could mean "honestly," "faithfully," "loyally," or "rightfully," as I have rendered it; the sense, I think, is "according to the laws of his own nature." Anyway, Cohen rewrites it in English to read: "The man who knows how to enjoy his existence as he ought has attained an absolute perfection, like that of the gods" (p. 406). To me this is not translation at all, but a lame paraphrase.

Most of the Penguins seem to me to suffer seriously from a flaw to some extent illustrated by this sample from Cohen's Montaigne selections: they all seem to assume that the entire responsibility of a translator, whatever the quirks and quiddities of his text, is fulfilled if he has put that text into a readable, familiar, everyday English. I am most grateful for their existence, but because of this serious limitation, whenever there are several alternatives to choose from for a given text, the Penguin, though rarely my last choice, is almost never my first.

To my mind, in trying to capture all one can of Montaigne, style as well as content, in English, the most persistent, often insoluble, problem is his wordplay, nearly all of which has recently been more precisely defined by a fine Italian critic as *annominatio,* the pairing (by close association, often juxtaposition) of words or phrases of similar sound but different meaning. I shall illustrate this copiously and conclude on this, for it is perhaps his most idiosyncratic trick of writing and permeates his essays, though not his letters, travel journal, and other writings that were not intended for publication.

Let me illustrate, as I promised, with some of these that I think I got more or less successfully and some I know I did not and about which I do not know whether that can be done. One I rendered to my satisfaction and much later was gratified to have noted with high praise by an eminent and attentive critic is from "Of Husbanding Your Will" (3:10, VS 1021–22, S 782). The passage that precedes and introduces it is this: "Les corps raboteux se sentent, les polis se manient imperceptiblement; la maladie se sent, la sante peu ou point" ("Rough bodies are felt, smooth ones are handled imperceptibly; sickness is felt, health little or not at all"); then comes the part that I like and that was well received: "ny les choses qui nous oignent, au pris de celles qui nous poignent," which I rendered thus: "nor do we feel the things that charm us, compared with those that harm us." That was an easy one, many are not, and some are in my view impossible. Consider this: "Je donnerois aussi volontiers mon sang que mon soing" (2:17, VS 642, S 417). ("I would give as willingly my blood as my care": to my mind, impossible.) A more complex one from near the end of "Vanity" (3:9, VS 994, S 761) I did not even attempt to imitate: "Je m'esgare, mais plustot par licence que par mesgarde." All I could do there was a fairly literal: "I go out of my way, but rather by license than carelessness." Another disturbing habit of Montaigne's is that of playing off against each other the third person singular present indicatives of *fuir* and *suivre,* as in "De la cruauté" (2:11, VS 429, S 313): "Je suy quelques vices, mais j'en fuy d'autres, autant qu'un sainct sçauroit faire." Here I ventured this: "I ply some vices, but I fly others as much as a saint could do." I thought of "pursue-eschew," but decided to eschew it. I think the English language will recover, and I *think* this is better here than just to say: "I follow certain vices, but I flee (or, avoid) others. . . ." And just one book later, in that lovely chapter "Of Cripples" (3:11, VS 1026, S 785), Montaigne gives us a one-two and then follows with a crusher. He was just now musing, he says, as he often does, on the vagueness and freedom of our reason; for he ordinarily sees that men, "aux faicts qu'on leur propose, s'amusent plus volontiers à en cercher la raison qu'à en cercher la verité: ils laissent là les choses, et s'amusent a traiter les causes." On that I could come up, however lamely, with this: "They leave aside the cases and amuse themselves treating the causes"; which I consider at least a good try. But when Montaigne (my friend! I thought) then lowered the boom with "Plaisants causeurs," which has still at least two meanings and then had in a sense three, I could only throw up my hands and put in a footnote, as I think any translator of a difficult author should sometimes do (not put them in the text, as Jacques Leclercq does in his Rabelais), much as an honest teacher must often tell students simply, "I don't know." (I put it down as "Comical prattlers," then took refuge at the bottom of the page in finer print.)

This *annominatio*, which Signora Garavini has shown to be a technique Montaigne learned from Seneca and may have been his main debt to him, is everywhere in the *Essais* and part of the fun of reading Montaigne. Strange as it seems (to me at least), none of the six earlier translators or eminent revisers (Florio, Cotton, Hazlitt [who revised Cotton], Ives, Trechmann, Zeitlin [a first-rate Montaigne scholar]) even attempted, as far as their translations show, to render this phenomenon. At least by attempting it I have given later translators a new problem to solve, a challenging new area to work on, and I am pleased to have done this and to have (I hope) solved satisfactorily as many as I have. The farthest I have strayed from the sense, at least in quest of one of these, is what I shall make bold to call "my fly-ply ploy." Most of those I attempted to reproduce or imitate I think I got less outlandishly than that, but the only one that I think back on with real pride and affection is one that I got only on my second try. If I overdid it, at least I did it. Let me close on that happy note. It comes late in that great chapter "Of Repentance" (3:2, VS 816, S 620), just before he says of his bodily life, "I have seen the grass, the flower, and the fruit; now I see the dryness—happily, since it is naturally," and immediately after: "If I had to live over again, I would live as I have lived." Here is the French: "ny je ne pleins le passé, ny je ne crains l'advenir." The sense is of course so rich that it does nicely without the rhyme, and when I first translated it, I settled, as I recall, for just that: "I neither lament the past nor fear the future." But coming back to it about fifteen years later I had to try for something better, and finally found what I hope is that: "I have neither tears for the past nor fears for the future."

In all these pages I have dealt almost solely with the problems I have seen in my practice of translation and my attempts to solve them or at least cope with them. But I trust my remarks have also made clear that for me it has long been, and continues to be, a pleasant undertaking that has given me many great pleasures.

"*ZIV,* THAT LIGHT": TRANSLATION
AND TRADITION IN PAUL CELAN
John Felstiner

Recently a letter of Paul Celan's from 1954 came to light, in which he admitted "shame and sadness" at having to abandon the project of translating Rilke and Gide's French correspondence into German.[1] Celan had wanted to begin "only after reading and re-reading Rilke's German letters," he said. But "this language can't simply be translated, it must be *translocated*" (*übersetzt . . . überge-setzt*). "I have hesitated for an unpardonably long time," Celan said, "translating and retranslating—with the unfortunate result that my doubts increased with each attempt." He hoped this correspondence would find its way into hands that have "no need to page endlessly through Rilke's German works before deciding to use this word or that; hands that can replace a semicolon with a period without hesitation."

Considering that Celan, with his wife Gisèle Lestrange, an artist, was living off such commissions at the time in Paris, and badly needed the money (shortly afterwards he did two novels by Simenon),[2] his scruples over Rilke speak all the more tellingly. They presume for translation an exhaustive sense of the entire oeuvre combined with a painstaking intimacy, all subject to the trials of revision and open at the same time to the venture of "transloca-tion."

If Rilke's French letters daunted him in the early fifties—as well they might, since he would be translating them into Rilke's own language—Celan still went on to do remarkable, often brilliant work in the art of translation: Valéry's *La Jeune Parque,* Rim-

John Felstiner is professor of English at Stanford University. He has translated extensively from the works of Paul Celan and Pablo Neruda. In *Translating Neruda: The Way to Macchu Picchu* (1980) he has reconstructed the various stages that led toward *Alturas de Macchu Picchu* and its verse translation.

This essay originated as a presentation to the Stanford Humanities Center narrative theory seminar, whose leader, Adena Rosmarin, I thank for that opportunity. It appeared in the Spring 1987 issue of *New Literary History*. I am especially grateful to Mary Lowenthal Felstiner for her rigorous and generous critique of the essay.

1. Letter to Renée Lang, Paris, 27 August 1954, in Jerry Glenn, "Three Letters," *Sulfur* 11 (1984): 27–31.
2. Paul Celan, *Gesammelte Werke,* ed. Beda Allemann and Stefan Reichert, with Rolf Bücher (Frankfurt: Suhrkamp, 1983) 4:864. This collected edition, in five volumes, is hereafter referred to as *GW.* All translations in the essay are my own.

baud, Char, Supervielle, Michaux, along with a dozen other French
poets, and Shakespeare, Dickinson, Frost, as well as Aleksandr
Blok, Sergei Esenin, and Osip Mandelshtam (*GW,* vols. 4 and 5).
Paul Celan never expressed himself fully or programmatically on
the question of translation. But he once said about Mandelshtam,
the Russian-Jewish poet hounded to death in 1938 whose poems
he translated as those of a blood brother and alter ego: "I consider
translating Mandelshtam to be as important a task as my own
verses."[3] Since Celan's own verses cost—and always almost
gained—him everything, that remark about Mandelshtam could
turn into a thoroughgoing mission for translation.

Translating Celan—translating any poet, in fact—appropriates
all the resources of interpretive criticism. Even more than that: in
translating, as in parody, critical and creative activity converge. The
fullest reading of a poem gets realized moment by moment in the
writing of a poem. So translation presents not merely a paradigm
but the utmost case of engaged literary interpretation.

Paul Celan's own poems themselves often take on the largest
tasks of translation, thereby enhancing his translator's task. A single
lyric may carry one tongue or text across to another, may gestate
within itself the epitome of a tradition, may reach from some certain past toward an uncertain yet open future. And while eight or
nine foreign languages crop up in Celan's writing, in no way does
he bring about a startling renascence of the word so much as when,
amid or after the German verses of a poem, he breaks into Hebrew
utterance.[4] Admittedly, that break would seem to raise twofold the
generic question of translation. For if lyric verse in the mother
tongue, especially verse as idiosyncratic as Celan's, resists the assim-
ilative process of translation, then Hebrew should create a double
strangeness, doubly resistant, doubly inalienable.

Yet doesn't the holy tongue specifically belong everywhere, at
any time, its persistent identity making translation impossible, even
uncalled for? Take for instance "Du sei wie du" ("You be like you";
GW 2:327), composed just before Celan's brief but intensive 1969
visit to Israel:

    3. Quoted in a letter (1975) from E. M. Raïs to Gleb Struve, in Victor Terras
and Karl S. Weimar, "Mandelstamm and Celan: A Postscript," *Germano-Slavica* 2, 5
(Spring 1978): 367.
    4. See John Felstiner, "Mother Tongue, Holy Tongue: On Translating and Not
Translating Paul Celan," *Comparative Literature* 38, 2 (Spring 1986): 113–36.

DU SEI WIE DU, immer.

Stant vp Jherosalem inde erheyff dich

Auch wer das Band zerschnitt zu dir hin,

inde wirt
erluchtet

knüpfte es neu, in der Gehugnis,
Schlammbrocken schluckt ich, im Turm,
Sprache, Finster-Lisene,

kumi
ori.

YOU BE LIKE YOU, ever.

Ryse vp Ierosalem and
rowse thyselfe

The very one who slashed the bond unto you,

and becum
yllumyned

knotted it new, in memoraunce,
spills of mire I swallowed, inside the tower,
speech, dark-buttress,

kumi
ori.

Celan's poem migrates back and forth between modern and medieval German, the medieval being Meister Eckhart's vernacular—
Stant vp Jherosalem . . . inde wirt erluchtet—for Saint Jerome's Vul-
gate of Isaiah 60:1, *Surge, illuminare, Jerusalem.*[5] Then this poem
closes by converting to the original Hebrew, the prophet's *kumi ori*
("Arise, shine").

    5. See Felstiner, "Translating Paul Celan's 'Du sei wie du,'" *Prooftexts* 3, 1
(1983): 91–108.

Merely to write in German means carrying on a tradition; for
Celan to write Meister Eckhart into his own verse practically seals
that tradition. But then he takes the miniature biography of "Du
sei wie du"—someone who slashed his bond to Jerusalem has renewed it in exile, through memory and speech—and makes this
story issue in biblical Hebrew. Such a trope leaves the poem slightly
but significantly at odds with the given tradition and turned toward
the imperative of another tradition. Celan's German listeners may
possibly recognize those Hebrew imperatives, *kumi ori*. More likely
they may not.

Still, the mother tongue was what he had. For Celan, his parents murdered and the Austrian-Jewish community and culture of
Bukovina destroyed by Nazi Germany, to go on writing in German
after 1945 meant paradoxically holding on to the thread of life.[6]
"Within reach, close and not lost," he later said, *nah und unverloren,*
"there remained in the midst of the losses this one thing: language.
This, the language, was not lost but remained, yes, in spite of
everything."[7] Yet this language, Celan insisted, had "passed
through the thousand darknesses of deathbringing speech." Toward the end of the war someone asked him why he did not begin
writing in Rumanian, the majority language he had learned at
school, or in French, which he knew quite well. "Only in the
mother tongue can one speak his own truth," Celan explained, "in
a foreign tongue the poet lies" (Chalfen, p. 148). Some years later
he was questioned by a Viennese bookseller in Paris about bilingualness. "I do not believe in bilingualness in poetry," he replied.
"Poetry—that is, the fateful uniqueness of language" (*GW* 3:175).
So this cleaving to the *Muttersprache* makes his recourse to Hebrew
in certain poems all the more pointed, and all the more fateful.

Franz Rosenzweig, in a 1921 letter to Gershom Scholem
about why he has reluctantly translated the Hebrew Grace after
Meals, speaks of his German-Jewish "predicament" in terms of the
need for translation. "As long as we speak German," Rosenzweig
says, "we cannot avoid this path that again and again leads us out

6. For a biography of Celan, see Israel Chalfen, *Paul Celan: Eine Biographie
seiner Jugend* (Frankfurt: Insel, 1979); Glenn, *Paul Celan* (New York: Twayne,
1973); Felstiner, "Paul Celan: The Strain of Jewishness," *Commentary* 79, 4 (April
1985): 44–55; and the most complete bibliographies to date: Christine Heuline's
in *Text u. Kritik*, 53–54, (2d ed., July 1984): 100–149, and Glenn's in *Studies in
Twentieth Century Literature* 8, 1 (Fall 1983): 129–58.

7. "Ansprache anlässlich der Entgegennahme des Literaturpreises der freien
Hansestadt Bremen" (1958; speech on receiving the Bremen Prize), in *GW* 3:185.

of what is alien and into our own."⁸ Paul Celan's "Du sei wie du,"
within the compass of eleven lines, leads from "what is alien and
into our own," from the choking mire of exile into earshot of Isaiah's messianic call, *kumi ori*. Whereas the medieval German stands
in a vernacular tradition and thus calls for an English equivalent,
those italics distinguishing *kumi ori* obviate the need to translate.
The Hebrew (and how many were left in Germany to recognize
Isaiah's words, which also occur in the Sabbath hymn "Lekha
dodi," summoning Israel to arise and shine?)—the Hebrew stands
as if at the beginning and the end of time, at the Babylonian exile
and the ultimate return to Zion, at once archaic and messianic.

Not many of Celan's lyrics come to rest with so clear a voice.
More often he will speak as in "Psalm" (*GW* 1:225) about

> our corona red
> from the purple-word we sang
> over, O over
> the thorn.

"That which happened," as Celan referred to the destruction of
European Jewry (*GW* 3:186), now prevents anything like the gratifying immediacy of lyric speech. No word can get to us except by
way of suffering and death: we sing "over, O over / the thorn."

To feel the force of translation in its fullest sense, I want to read
quite slowly and consider translating an even shorter lyric than "Du
sei wie du"—namely, the twenty-three words disposed over ten
lines beginning "Nah, im Aortenbogen" (1967; *GW* 2:202):

> NAH, IM AORTENBOGEN,
> im Hellblut:
> das Hellwort.
>
> Mutter Rahel
> weint nicht mehr.
> Rübergetragen
> alles Geweinte.

8. Letter to Gershom Scholem, 10 March 1921, in Franz Rosenzweig, *Briefe und Tagebücher* 2 (1918–29), ed. Rachel Rosenzweig and Edith Rosenzweig Scheinmann (The Hague: Martinus Nijhoff, 1979), p. 699.

Still, in den Kranzarterien,
unumschnürt:
Ziw, jenes Licht.

CLOSE, IN THE AORTIC ARCH,
in the bright blood:
the bright word.

Mother Rachel
weeps no more.
Carried across,
all that was wept.

Quiet, in the coronary arteries,
unconstricted:
Ziv, that light.

Nah, "near," "close" in space or time, not distant, not long to await:
the poem opens here and now on a single syllable, an adjective with
no noun or verb modifying the poise of the word. In a way, this
initial syllable countervails everything previous, everything about
us that until now has not been "nigh"—everything distant, displaced, sundered, estranged.

   To unfold Paul Celan's poem word by word, or say, moment
by moment, means releasing it into the dimension of time and thus
into a way of fulfillment. Yet before this poem moves on from its
first moment, *Nah,* it harks back (in my ears, at least) to something
Celan had written ten years before, a poem he called "Tenebrae"
(1957; *GW* 1:163), which began,

Nah sind wir, Herr,
nahe und greifbar.

Close by, Lord, we are
close and claspable.

Having subscribed to the rubric of Tenebrae, that sacred office
darkening into Christ's Passion, Celan's poem then exposes another
passion:

Clasped already, Lord,
clawed into each other as though
each of our bodies were
your body, Lord.

Not Golgotha now but the gas chamber—human being so broken
that it throws down divinity:

Pray, Lord,
pray to us,
we are close,

wir sind nah. "Warped," says the speaker, we went "To the water
trough" and found "It was blood, it was / what you shed, Lord."
Possibly the desperate irony marking Christ's blood here in
"Tenebrae" can be heard giving way to "bright blood" and a
"bright word" in the later poem, "Nah, im Aortenbogen." There is
no doubt that in "Tenebrae," in its opening lines themselves—
"Nah sind wir, Herr, nahe und greifbar"—Celan was summoning
a far earlier voice, Friedrich Hölderlin and the opening of "Patmos":

Nah ist
Und schwer zu fassen der Gott.
Wo aber Gefahr ist, wächst
Das Rettende auch.

Close by
and hard to grasp is the God.
Yet where danger is, grows
What rescues as well.

After this, Hölderlin's hymn makes its way from Saint John, Christ,
and the disciples, to divine scripture, and finally to God the Father's solicitude for "German song." So, what made Hölderlin a
tremendous presiding spirit for Paul Celan also made him an impossible exemplar. No saving grace of a God "close by and hard to
grasp" was to fall upon those "close and claspable" Jews "clawed
into each other" at Sobibor, Chelmno, Maidanek, Treblinka, and
Auschwitz.

One would have to trace Germany's Christian-Jewish history
as refracted in romantic through expressionist poetry in order to
spark the distance between "Patmos" and "Tenebrae," between *Nah*
spoken by Hölderlin and eventually by Celan. "In the beginning
was the Word, and the Word was with God, and the Word was
God. . . . In him was life, and the life was the light of men" (John
1:1–4). By the time this dispensation has descended two millennia

to a Central European boy who in 1934, just after becoming Bar
Mitzvah, told his aunt recently emigrated to Palestine: "Why, as for
antisemitism in our school, I could write a 300-page opus about
it" (Chalfen, p. 51); by the time *das Wort* has descended from John
through Luther to Hölderlin and then has "passed through its own
answerlessnesses," as Celan put it, "passed through a frightful mut-
ing, passed through the thousand darknesses of deathbringing
speech" (*GW* 3:186)—by this time God's life- and light-bringing
Word sounds barely audible and asks the keenest ear.

And yet, through the word *nah*, "near," another theological
line led down to Celan, which he might have grasped. In several
psalms, "The Lord is nigh unto them that are of a broken heart"
(34:18), or salvation is nigh. And in Deuteronomy 30:14, to as-
sure the people that His commandments are not beyond their
reach, the Lord says, "For the word is very near to you, in your
mouth and in your heart, that you may do it." This might almost
serve as epigraph to the poem I am translating.

"Nah, im Aortenbogen": so much depends, for Celan, upon
each word in turn, that I want to respect as exactly as possible the
timing of his verse, the length and pulse of this opening line:
"Close, in the aorta's arch." (I wish I might use "Nigh," both for
the biblicism and the vowel tone leading to "bright." But Celan's
Nah does not sound archaic and moves right into something actual.) It is the heart's pulse, the beat of the blood, we are beginning
to feel here. Possibly I should respect a scientific term and say "aortic" rather than "aorta's" arch. After all, Celan had his reasons for
preferring precise, undistorted language in German. Yet I also want
a purely physical sense of the arch of the aorta, that turning point
where blood oxygenated by the lungs begins recirculating to the
body.

Because a point in time as well as space occurs "in the aorta's
arch," Celan's first stanza holds its poise by setting a colon in place
of a verb, and simply marking

    im Hellblut:
    das Hellwort.

Here, if I omit a definite article, the pulse holds precisely in English, marking

    in bright blood:
    the bright word.

But why cling to a criterion of rhythmic measure? Just *because*, one wants to say—because such taut and terse lines have no breath to spare, and again, because time seems of the essence in this lyric. We do not yet know what "bright word" lies "close, in the aorta's arch," poised strongly by the colon and line break after "bright blood." Maybe the originating logos itself, the word that became flesh? "Das ist mein Blut," Jesus says, "This is my blood" (Matthew 26:28). Celan's opening stanza carries overtones of New Testament language, but somehow it seems more important that we do not yet know what word this is, and until we do, it seems best to keep time, keeping to the pulse of these few syllables.

What then of the adjective *hell*, meaning "clear" or "bright"? This blood is both clear, purified of carbon dioxide, and bright red, aerated with oxygen. Possibly Celan's word *Hellblut* echoes an earlier poem of his which describes a children's song that despite the European Jewish catastrophe "stayed motherly, summery, bright- / blooded," *hellblütig*.[9] Doubtless my choice of "bright" means to anticipate "that light" at the end of the poem. And perhaps after all it is enough to say that "bright blood," following upon the doubled *a*'s in "aorta's arch," makes a satisfying sound.

In the endless to-and-fro of translating, I have found that by studying Celan's own practice as a translator, I can identify more clearly his essential practice as a poet.[10] What happens in his versions of Shakespeare, Dickinson, and Frost, for instance—the Germans say these poets are *Celanisiert*, "Celanified"—also happens in Celan's own verse as well. His translations, compared to their originals, tend toward compression and repetition, and thus toward parataxis; and in translating he does not hesitate to restructure or invent. Having spotted these habits, I can then look again at "Nah, im Aortenbogen" as if it were for one uncanny moment Celan's rendering of some American lyric, something beginning like this perhaps:

> The red blood flows
> into the aortic arch
> with a bright word.

9. "In der Luft," *GW* 1:290.

10. See Leonard Moore Olschner, *Der feste Buchstab: Erläuterungen zu Paul Celans Gedichtübertragungen* (Göttingen: Vandenhoeck & Ruprecht, 1985), a superb book to which I am greatly indebted.

These fairly insipid lines now show how striking Celan has made
it:

> Nah, im Aortenbogen,
> im Hellblut:
> das Hellwort.

And they show the need for an English version moved responsibly
by Celan's turns of speech.

Thanks to the kindredness of English to German, Celan's next two
lines also come across perfectly intact in syllable and accent:

> Mutter Rahel
> weint nicht mehr.

> Mother Rachel
> weeps no more.

In forming what will turn out to be the poem's only independent
clause, they make a firm narrative claim, which again has to do with
time: something that used to happen, now no longer does. The
present tense at the poem's midpoint, *weint,* balances the poem at
an ever-present turning point. This says we may always know an
end to weeping, but may always need one, too: ambiguous news,
making us look back into the palimpsest of the sentence, "Mother
Rachel weeps no more."

We go back and touch first, as most of Celan's audience would,
upon the New Testament, so called, the Gospel according to Matthew (2:17–18) on the Slaughter of the Innocents, where it is said,
"Then was fulfilled that which was spoken by Jeremy the prophet,
saying, In Rama was there a voice heard, lamentation, and weeping, and great mourning, Rachel weeping for her children, and
would not be comforted, because they are not." But the Christ
child is saved. "Prefiguring" this event, in the Old Testament as
Matthew sees it, six centuries earlier we now find Jeremiah (31:15)
lamenting Israel's Babylonian exile: "Thus saith the Lord; A voice
was heard in Ramah, lamentation, and bitter weeping; Rachel
weeping for her children." But the people return into Zion, for
God renews His covenant made long before that in the mythic past
with Jacob, husband of Rachel, the matriarch of the tribes of Israel,

as recounted in the book of Genesis, whose Hebrew title, *Bereshit,* means "In the beginning." We have returned to the beginning that was quietly prompted by a poem saying "Mother Rachel / weeps no more." This return prepares quite another sort of fulfillment and redemption than the Gospel imagines.

Tradition, the receiving and that which is received, in Hebrew *Kabbalah,* speaks of Mother Rachel as a figure of the Shekhinah, God's luminous presence dwelling within the world. Wherever the tribes of Israel are exiled or suffering, she weeps and entreats God's mercy. Celan knew this legend, perhaps from childhood, perhaps later. On May 3, 1967, he read Gershom Scholem's essay on the Shekhinah,[11] and within a week wrote "Nah, im Aortenbogen." Cool-headed commentators point out that Celan's Judaism came mediated through Scholem and Buber. That is only partly true, and anyway in Celan this Judaism becomes immediate. The tradition handed him what he knew already, and often what he knew to his grief. Long before adopting the image of Mother Rachel lamenting her children, he composed an elegy to his own mother, murdered by the S.S. in a Ukrainian labor camp. "Aspen Tree" (1945; *GW* 1:19) has one couplet that runs:

> Rain cloud, do you linger over the well?
> My soft-voiced mother weeps for everyone,

"Meine leise Mutter weint für alle." So in 1967 Celan's poem, "Close, in the aorta's arch," receives and recirculates a tradition that can bind his own plight into that of his people, in a single phrase intimating continuity ("Mother Rachel") and redemption ("weeps no more").

I was startled to find in Celan's copy of Scholem's essay on the Shekhinah, at the bottom of the page that speaks of Mother Rachel weeping for her exiled children, some pencilled Yiddish lines from a popular song:[12]

11. In Scholem, *Von der mystischen Gestalt der Gottheit* (Zurich: Rhein-Verlag, 1962), pp. 136–91. For this and subsequent material relating to Celan's library and reading, I am deeply grateful to Gisèle Celan-Lestrange.

12. From Moyshe Leyb Halpern, "Night," 11, in *In New York* (1919). I am indebted to Robert Freedman and Kathryn Hellerstein for help in identifying these lines, which I have transliterated.

Vet di mama Rokhl veynen
Vet Meshiekh nit mer kenen
Dos geveyn aribertrogn.

The sturdy rhyme and beat do not translate easily:

If Mama Rachel starts to weep
Messiah can't still bear to keep
Us waiting here and weeping so.

Evidently Scholem's discussion touched off this memory in Celan, and thus a yearning, attuned to the consolations and compensations of Diaspora Judaism. Now set these Yiddish lines alongside the middle stanza of "Nah, im Aortenbogen": they point up a messianic change of heart, and they make a difference to the translator, too. Instead of the old familiar song's conditional, anticipatory form, now in Celan's lyric "Mother Rachel weeps no more." And where the Yiddish *aribertrogn* means "bear," "endure," Celan draws on another sense of that verb which has its German counterpart in *herübertragen*, "carry across." Everything that was wept, *alles Geweinte*, is now not "borne with" but "borne across," transferred, perhaps translated, even transformed.

As a four-line stanza set between two three-line stanzas, the quatrain contains its own central turning point that is the poem's as well:

Mother Rachel
weeps no more.
Carried across,
all that was wept.

This turning actually takes the form of a trope, a metaphor—the metaphor at the very root of the idea of metaphor: *Rübergetragen*, "carried across." Celan had a favored word for such critical moments: *Atemwende*, "breath-turning."[13] It figures in his great apology for poetry, "The Meridian" (1960), and as the title of a book. Here in his poem, "Close, in the aorta's arch," the breath turns as the blood returns, in a moment of renewal.

A draft of this poem has *Hinübergetragen* with "Hin" crossed

---

13. "Der Meridian," *GW* 3:195, 200; *Atemwende*, *GW* 2:7.

out and "R" put in to make *Rübergetragen*. That way Celan not only prolongs the stanza's basic tempo, stressing the first syllable in each line:

> Mutter Rahel
> weint nicht mehr.
> Rübergetragen
> alles Geweinte.

He also voices a colloquialism (*rüber* for "across," rather than *hinüber* or *herüber*) which I'm told he liked hearing on the street in Germany.[14] What's more, this expedient change for rhythm and sound may embody an essential change as well: *hinüber* would have meant the weeping was carried over "there, thither," giving this poem a utopian thrust as Celan's adverbs of direction so often do. But *rüber* might also stand for *herüber*, which would translate the weeping "here," toward the speaker. Some kind of crossing has occurred, and though no "I" actually situates a speaker in this poem, possibly the nuance on *rüber* hints that for a moment at least, he is where he wants to be—not distant but close, not displaced but at home.

That one word *Rübergetragen* seems compact with all the Jewish people's crossings, their founding moments: Abraham out of Ur to Canaan, Moses through the Red Sea to Sinai, Joshua across the Jordan into the Promised Land, the Israelites back from Babylon to Zion—as the Lord says in Jeremiah 31:15, comforting Rachel, "Thy children shall come back to their own border." (The word "Hebrew" itself, *Ivri*, means "he who crossed over.") And a poem composed in late spring 1967 might also reflect that modern passage to Jerusalem's Old City and Temple wall.

Again, because so much seems at stake here, I feel bound almost liturgically to keep the measure of this stanza. Originally Celan placed *alles* in line 3, so that it ran: *Rübergetragen alles / Geweinte*. By giving *Rübergetragen* a line to itself, he shaped a firm, equal cadence in the second half of the stanza, alternating two- and three-syllable feet:

> Rübergetragen
> alles Geweinte.

---

14. Conversation, Renate Böschenstein-Schäfer, 15 October 1984.

Carried across here,
all of that weeping.

In trying for a version faithful to its source and inspiration, I see
translation as a carrying across not so much in space, from one
nation's tongue to another's, as in time, from generation to
(re)generation. Perhaps for *Rübergetragen*, "Carried across now"
may say even more than "Carried across here." This poem in particular asks for fidelity because Celan's lines themselves are conveying and renewing something precious—a "bright word" as yet un-
pronounced, and a messianic legend. He himself adopts a rather
uncommon German noun, *Geweinte*, which first of all echoes his
earlier elegy to the Jewish dead, "The Vintagers" (1954): "They
harvest the wine of their eyes, / they tread all that was wept," *alles
Geweinte* (*GW* 1:140). For the 1967 poem, although my phrase
"all of that weeping" matches Celan's meter, it misses a crucial element: the pastness of that weeping. But "all the old weeping,"
which satisfies sense and meter alike, seems slightly excessive. Perhaps, "all the years' weeping"? Whatever the translator's difficulties,
Celan's uncommon word *Geweinte* nonetheless keeps quite close to
the common Yiddish word *geveyn*, "lament," from the song about
Rachel that he remembered and that his poem transforms.

Now not only time but translation itself seems of the essence
in this lyric. *Rübergetragen* may even hint at such an idea, since the
verb *übertragen*, literally "to carry over" or "across," also signifies a
mode of literary translation that does not merely replicate—*über-
setzen*—but re-creates, something like Celan "translocating" Rilke's
French letters. (As it happens, *übertragen* can also mean "trans-
fuse," an apt image for "Nah, im Aortenbogen.") Finally, then, with
the second half of Celan's middle stanza, keeping rhythmic identity
in English means trying a freer version:

Rübergetragen
alles Geweinte.

Carried across now,
all the years' weeping.

Especially the word "now," replicating Celan's line length with a
fifth syllable, finds something slightly new to say in translation—
and finds it not just expedient but essential, I hope.

The word "now," my attempt at tuning in to Celan a little more
finely, quickens our expectation of his closing stanza:

> Still, in den Kranzarterien,
> unumschnürt:
> Ziw, jenes Licht.

And this rhythm recalls an earlier one. In the moment before we
begin to grasp (or translate) what the three lines are saying, we see
already how they tally physically with Celan's opening lines:

> Nah, im Aortenbogen,
> im Hellblut:
> das Hellwort.

That strong pause after the first monosyllable, followed by a prep-
ositional phrase, then three syllables up to a colon: in both stanzas
these elements lead to a third line announcing something that even
by the end of the poem may not be quite clear to us. But clearly
"the bright word" has come round to be spoken: *Ziw*, or phonetically in English, *Ziv*. Celan's last stanza carries on from the first,
with something new: rooted change, the lifeblood of tradition.

First *Nah* and now *Still*: given the syntax of each stanza, a
"bright word" is "close" and now—what? "Silent"? Yes, that
stressed *i* resonates nicely with "light" at the end, like the German
Still and *Licht*. But I need a word meaning motionless as well as
soundless. "Quiet"? yes, that would do, but the symmetry between
Nah and *Still* requires an adjective of one syllable. "Calm"?
"Hushed"? The wrong overtones. Then why not "still" itself? The
adjective fits beautifully, and also we can hear the adverb "still" (or,
less usefully, the conjunction "neverthless"). Keats's Grecian urn,
Eliot's music in *Four Quartets* offer rich precedents for a grammatical ambiguity on "still" that reconciles mortal time with spiritual—an ambiguity I think Celan's poem also presents us with. Yet
still in German has no sense of something prolonged, enduring—
ought I to add that idea? Am I really adding it, though, when the
poem itself speaks of a word that has been refreshed, a mother no
longer weeping, something borne across and unconstricted? All
these bespeak a process carrying right up to the present tense of
the poem. Celan once described a certain line of his verse as having
after many years "remained true" and thus "become true," *wahrge-*

bliebene, wahrgewordene.[15] Maybe the same holds for that "bright word."

Finally it is stillness, quiet, calm that matters, after crossing over from exile and lament. "Close, in the aorta's arch," the word now goes "Still, in the coronary arteries." Even physiologically some movement has occurred, since freshened blood first pumps through the aorta and only then into the coronary arteries that wreathe and sustain the heart. We have a vivified stillness, then. To specify this change, proper nomenclature seems called for in translating *Kranzarterien.* And as so often with Celan, the technical term engenders something extra through its literal sense. So if "coronary" unfortunately drags out the rhythm—I would prefer something like the "heart's own" or even the "wreathing" arteries—our word "coronary" does embody a corona or wreath of light (*Lichtkranz* in German) that can be glimpsed here and that helps bring home the circle moving through this poem.

What was unstill has turned still, and what was entwined, enlaced, corded round, has become *unumschnürt.* A word *Umschnürung* exists (though it is not the usual term) for "tourniquet," so perhaps some angina of a sort, some strangling or angst, has been released. For *unumschnürt,* "unconstricted" would pick up assonance from "still," but a more striking and concrete trisyllable, "unbinded," will echo in (our word for) the poem's final word— "light."

Ziw, jenes Licht, "Ziw, that light"—is that all there is to it? For simply arriving at an English version, yes, I suppose so. But while this poem draws to its close, or while Paul Celan draws his poem round to its close, questions open up that affect even the simplest translation and that test the idea of translation itself. What does *Ziw* mean? Where did he find it? Why spell it that way? Should one render the word at all? And does *Ziw* truly correspond to *Licht* or "light"?

To answer such questions, to find my way toward what may after all be an inevitable translation of the last line, means again going back into the past of this poem and this poet. In late May 1960, Celan took his wife and son to Zurich to meet Nelly Sachs. For twenty years since her last-minute flight from Berlin to Stockholm, she had not set foot on German soil but had devoted herself, writ-

ing like Celan in her mother tongue, to the "suffering of Israel."
When a major German prize was awarded her, Sachs elected to stay
in Zurich and cross the Bodensee to receive it.[16] Celan came from
Paris to greet her.
She and Celan had taken comfort and courage from each other's poetry over the years, so this first encounter touched them
acutely. They talked, he wrote in a poem four days later, of "cloud-
ing through clarity," *Trübung durch Helles,*[17] and he expressed his
bleaker sense of the Jewish tragedy:

> Our talk was of your God, I spoke
> against him, I
> let the heart that I had,
> hope:
> for
> his highest, deathrattled, his
> wrangling word.

But his poem notes something else that happened as they sat looking over the Limmat River at Zurich's great cathedral:

> On the day of an ascension, the
> Minster stood over there, it came
> with some gold across the water.

It was forty days after Easter, the cathedral shimmering toward
them "with some gold," and that gold, in a mere subordinate
phrase, made a different miracle than Christ ascending into heaven:
it made a shining these two survivors witnessed together. On her
way back from Zurich, Sachs visited the Celan family in Paris, and
"as we spoke a second time about God," he writes her in a letter
that summer, again "the golden gleam stood on the wall."[18] But by
this time Nelly Sachs, her memories of Nazism revived by the re-

16. Ehrhard Bahr, *Nelly Sachs* (Munich: Beck, 1980), p. 52.
17. "Zürich, Zum Störchen," *GW* 1:214. For the date of the poem, see Otto
Pöggeler, "Kontroverses zur Ästhetik Paul Celans (1920–1970)," *Zeitschrift für Ästhetik und allgemeine Kunstwissenschaft* 25, 2 (1980): 220.
18. See Bahr, "Paul Celan und Nelly Sachs: Ein Dialog in Gedichten," in
Chaim Shoham and Bernd Witte, eds., *Datum und Zitat bei Paul Celan* (Bern: Peter
Lang, 1987), pp. 183–94; and Celan, "Briefe an Nelly Sachs," in Werner Hamacher
and Winfried Menninghaus, eds., *Paul Celan* (Frankfurt: Suhrkamp, 1988), pp.
14–19.

JOHN FELSTINER

cent trip, had fallen into a terrifying persecution mania. Celan
wrote generous, jocular, heartening letters: "Look, Nelly. Look, it's
getting light [*hell*] . . . You're breathing free,"and he welcomed her
new "brightnesses" (*Helligkeiten*). He even journeyed to Stockholm to visit her in the hospital. Then off and on throughout the
sixties, Celan himself was afflicted with an anxiety fueled in part by
German neo-Nazism and recrudescent antisemitism.[19]
    Now what does *Ziw* mean? Where did he find it? First of all,
the word occurs in a Sabbath evening song, "Yedid nefesh" ("Beloved soul"). Celan may or may not have remembered this song.
In May 1967, he was given one of Gershom Scholem's books on
Jewish mysticism and read it immediately, with minute attentive-
ness. Scholem's chapter on the Shekhinah, after mentioning
Mother Rachel weeping for her exiled children, says that God's
indwelling presence "can reveal itself in an unearthly brightness—
this is often called the light (*Ziw*) of the Shekhinah" (Scholem, p.
143). Celan underlined this sentence and wrote *Ziw* at the bottom
of the page; not only that, on the book's endleaf he wrote "p. 143
Ziw," and finding *Ziw* missing in Scholem's index, he carefully in-
serted it with its page number, in all these ways marking the sali-
ence of a word that he had been waiting for, and that had been
waiting for him, seven years since seeing the golden gleam with
Nelly Sachs.
    Just as the word at the heart of "Nah, im Aortenbogen" was
vouchsafed to Celan, so was the body of his poem. In May 1967,
he happened to be reading a recently published handbook of human physiology, with graphic detail on the various organs and
functions.[20] A section on "the most important arteries" describes
the aortic arch and the coronary arteries, speaks of *hellrotes Blut*,
"bright red blood," and tells how to deal with a wound: press the
artery, then put on an *Umschnürung*, a tourniquet. From this con-
fluence of a technical manual and a study of the Shekhinah, I believe, came "Nah, im Aortenbogen," a draft of which Celan actually
wrote on the inside cover of the physiology book, one week after
reading Scholem.
    Whatever *Ziw* means—for the poem does not really say—it

19. See Felstiner, "Paul Celan: The Strain of Jewishness" and "The Biography
of a Poem," *New Republic* 2 (April 1984): 27–31.
    20. A. Faller, *Der Körper des Menschen: Einführung in Bau und Funktion* (Stutt-
gart: Georg Thieme, 1966).

must be the *Hellwort* announced in stanza one. Within the twenty
seconds it takes to speak these verses, the poem creates its own
internal time, enough for prefiguring and fulfilling "the bright
word" *Ziw.* Toward the end of 1967, Celan wrote to Nelly Sachs
about the light they'd seen together: "Once, in a poem, there also
came to me, by way of the Hebrew, a name for it" (Hamacher and
Menninghaus, p. 18). He often experienced this kind of déjà vu,
coming upon some item new to him—a fact, a word, a biblical or
other citation—that nonetheless confirmed something he had already expressed in his poetry. Possibly it made him feel rooted
within an organic tradition when a name for that golden light in
Zurich and Paris came to him, as he says, "by way of the Hebrew,"
as if the language had been holding a spiritual identity in store for
him.

Although Celan tapped many other Judaic sources, *Ziw* definitely bears the mark of Gershom Scholem, who has recovered
the Jewish mystical tradition for this century. Scholem employed
an idiosyncratic (and not always consistent) transliteration,[21] so
that here the Hebrew זי״ו (*zayin-yud-vav*), in English *Ziv*, should
phonetically be *Siw* in German. Scholem made it *Ziw* and Celan
followed him. (Whether Celan knew the proper Hebrew pronunciation, I am not sure. In any case, an American translator has
heard Celan's *Ziw* with a German Z and thus in his version transliterated it *Tsiv*,[22] which makes the word unduly strange.) Depend-
ing upon what valence attaches to this esoteric term, spelling may
or may not matter much. Why, for instance, did Celan not set it in
italics like nearly all the other Hebrew and Yiddish in his poetry?
Perhaps because this word now felt close, internal to his writing,
not strange but at home. Whatever the reason, any reader-
translator not versed in Jewish lore faces something impenetrable
in *Ziv.*

Should one render the Hebrew at all? No, certainly not if Celan had distinguished and preserved it with italics, as I have felt
drawn to do in my version. But his whole poem is in the same
typeface, all of a piece, so that we read along expecting to understand *Ziv* in its turn. In fact we do not readily understand the word.

21. To Scholem's *Von der mystischen Gestalt,* where the Hebrew character *zayin*
is transliterated with *Z,* compare his *Die jüdische Mystik in ihren Hauptströmungen*
(Frankfurt: Alfred Metzner, 1957), which transliterates *zayin* with *S.*
22. Joachim Neugroschel, trans., "Four Poems by Paul Celan," *Midstream* 23,
8 (October 1977): 46.

Lighting upon it after a colon, syntactically symmetric to *das Hell-wort*, we know we are now hearing "the bright word" but we still feel slightly expectant, awaiting a final clarity. To translate *Ziv* would dissipate that sense of half-concealed revelation. And anyway, what could possibly render this unearthly brightness? The usual bulky paraphrase, "divine effulgence," shows that not merely rhythm and idiom but truth itself demands an absolute identity in translation rather than a paraphrase.

We must not because we can not translate *Ziv*. Having emerged from within one people's singular experience of exile and expectation, it has no equivalent in Christian mysticism. What's more, the sacred nature of the written and spoken word in Hebraic tradition—to alter scripture condemns the world to chaos—would forbid the possibility of equivalence. In such a word as *Ziv*, letter and spirit are not separable, as ordinarily they must be for translation to occur. Especially in Kabbalah, divine speech created the world—"God said, Let there be light" (אור, *Or*)—and that speech being Hebrew, the "bright word" *Ziv* patently identifies and even incarnates what no other word can. So let it be.

Ziv surprises us with a specifically Hebrew (though originally Aramaic) voice amid German verse. In the aftermath of an *Endlösung*, a "final solution" that invented words and ways to make Europe *judenrein*, "pure of Jews," Celan's poem breaks into Hebrew—or say that Hebrew breaks into the poem—with a final and purifying force. For that reason alone, for the fact that Jews uttered Hebrew at the cost of their lives (and at the moment of their deaths), one wants to leave this word intact, not translate it. The course of the poem itself actually translates *das Hellwort* into *Ziv*, as the aorta brings freshened blood to nourish the heart. German converting to Hebrew: a radical conversion that the *Ziv* of my version can suggest but that inevitably loses its historical force in the poem's American setting.

Celan, writing in his mother tongue that was the murderers' tongue, knew well enough that a German audience no longer held more than a handful of people who might recognize the Hebrew at the end of this poem. ("The landscape from which I come to you may be unfamiliar to most of you," he said to a Bremen audience in 1958 [*GW* 3:185]. "It is the landscape that was home to a not inconsiderable part of those Hasidic stories that Martin Buber has retold for us all in German.") So perhaps Celan actively wished his poem to occult for a moment: let his German listeners, for whatever good it may do them, stumble on the Hebrew and fail to understand—that does not in the least diminish its authenticity and its necessity. Indeed why not even use a Hebrew font for the word? This would not have strained the resources of Suhrkamp Verlag, and Celan was a prize in their showcase. Possibly he wanted *Ziw* refractory but not utterly baffling. Or possibly, having shunned his father's Zionist leanings before Nazism killed both his parents, and now having not yet journeyed to Israel, Celan felt unready or unworthy to make use of Hebrew, the father tongue, the reclaimed language spoken at last on its native soil. The act of translation in "Nah, im Aortenbogen" had not carried him quite that far across.

Taking this thought even further, I wonder what would become of *Ziw* in a Hebrew version of the poem.[23] Certainly far more readers of such a version would recognize the term *Ziv*, but they would lose that sudden change of tongue, that heartlifting turn of breath from German to Hebrew. We commonly lament the "loss in translation." Here a stranger kind of loss would occur, strange because invisible—which is tantamount to saying that Paul Celan ineluctably wrote in and for the Diaspora. In 1948, having migrated from Bukovina, his homeland, to Bucharest, Vienna, and finally Paris, he wrote to relatives in the new state of Israel: "Perhaps I am one of the last who must live out to the end the destiny of the Jewish spirit in Europe."[24] Many of Celan's poems enact that destiny, perhaps every last one of them does. And the poems with Hebrew in them, especially with Hebrew at the end, pointedly enact the Diaspora condition of exile and messianic expectation.

When Celan visited Israel in October 1969, he reunited with childhood friends and other survivors who had emigrated directly there. He recited his poems in German, and heard Hebrew versions of some of them.[25] For a good friend in Jerusalem he wrote out "Du sei wie du," but when he came at the end to Isaiah's *kumi ori,*

23. See Celan, *Shoshanat Haayin,* trans. Manfred Winkler, Afterword by Israel Chalfen (Tel Aviv: Sifriat Poalim, 1983). "Die Schleuse" ("The Sluice") is translated there (see below), but not "Nah, im Aortenbogen." See also Celan, *Dvar-ma Yihyeh,* ed. Ben-Zion Orgad (Tel Aviv: Sifriat Poalim, 1987), which includes "Du sei wie du."

24. Quoted in Bianca Rosenthal, "Quellen zum frühen Paul Celan: Der Alfred Margul-Sperber-Nachlass in Bukarest," *Zeitschrift für Kulturaustausch* 3 (1982): 230.

25. See Chalfen, "Paul Celan in Jerusalem," *Die Stimme,* November 1969, p. 5, and Gershom Schocken, "Paul Celan in Tel Aviv," *Neue Rundschau* 91, 2:3 (1980): 256–59.

"Arise, shine," he naturally used Hebrew script rather than the transliteration his published version contains.[26] Celan in Israel responded intensely and gratefully to the complex of land, people, monuments, language. But he did not remain there; he returned for good to Paris and to his writing. "Poetry—that is, the fateful uniqueness of language," he had once said (*GW* 3:175). Like the German poems of his that are offset by Hebrew, in the Promised Land he would have lost something in translation.

"The darkness of exile flows from forgetfulness, and in remembrance is the secret of redemption." That saying from the Baal Shem Tov, the eighteenth-century founder of Hasidism, can illuminate Celan's discovery in Scholem and his writing of "Nah, im Aortenbogen." For the poem marks a passage from estrangement to closeness, and in *Ziw* is the secret of redemption. Yet the Hebrew does not bring this poem to its end. *Ziw, jenes Licht:* if it were not for *jenes*, the demonstrative "that"—if Celan had simply said *Ziw, das Licht*—then he would only be translating for us: "*Ziv,* the light." Instead, saying "that light" does not really translate but throws us back on the Hebrew word and gestures toward something ineffable that possibly we have experienced. For the reader with ideal recall, *jenes Licht* can summon up Zurich in May 1960, so possibly this 1967 poem ends by intimately addressing Nelly Sachs: You remember, Nelly—*that* light! At the same time, Celan's gesture in the closing line, "*Ziv,* that light," returns us to a certain light—not to Saint John's *logos,* which was "In the beginning . . . the light of men," but to *Ziv haShekhinah,* a radiance attending Israel even in the darkness of exile.

Celan abstains from translating *Ziv* because the very moment of merely speaking that "bright word" fulfills an act of translation. In arriving at *Ziv,* the poem like our lifeblood has described a meridian and now rests for a moment in Hebrew, the old-new language spoken in the beginning and perennially, millennially charged with expectation. I say "meridian" because Celan loved that figure, using it to entitle his major speech on poetry and whenever some idea, image, or experience of his own suddenly linked up to an earlier one in Kafka, say, or Mandelshtam. Particularly in periods of bleakness he saw his life and writing both drawn along

26. See Felstiner, "Translating Paul Celan's 'Jerusalem' Poems," *Religion and Literature* 16, 1 (Winter 1984): 37–47.

the meridian of exile and return—a return in spirit to his childhood homeland, and a turning to Jewish sources. What he says at the end of "The Sluice" (1960; *GW* 1:222) holds true in effect for every poem he wrote:

To
poly-goddedness
I lost a word that sought me:
Kaddish.

Through
the sluice I had to go,
to salvage the word back into
and out of and across the salt flood:
Yizkor.

With *Kaddish,* a prayer for the dead often recited by the surviving son, and *Yizkor,* denoting the memorial service, Celan ends these stanzas by remembering the Hebrew for remembering the dead.

In Tel Aviv in 1969, Celan told the Hebrew Writers Association, "I have come to you here in Israel because I needed to" (*GW* 3:203). And he commented deliberately on their revived tongue: "I take joy in every newly won, self-feelingful, fulfilled word that rushes up to strengthen those who are turned toward it." A few of Celan's lyrics, such as "Nah, im Aortenbogen," are turned toward the Hebrew language in somewhat the way that Walter Benjamin saw the "Angelus Novus" of Paul Klee, the angel of history, facing the past but irresistibly drawn toward the future.[27]

I see the same meridian moving through Celan's language of memory as through Jewish messianic thinking itself. In Karl Kraus's phrase, cited by Benjamin: "Origin is the goal."[28] For a people as for a person in exile, the old words count—having "remained true," they are "become true," in Celan's formula (*GW* 1:220). And for the Kabbalists, as Scholem says, "Speech reaches God because it comes from God."[29] Remembering, recognizing,

27. Benjamin, "Geschichtsphilosophische Thesen," IX, in *Schriften,* ed. T. W. Adorno and Gretel Adorno (Frankfurt: Suhrkamp, 1955), 1:499. For a translation, see Benjamin, *Illuminations,* ed. Hannah Arendt, trans. Harry Zohn (New York: Schocken, 1969), pp. 257–58.
28. Benjamin, "Geschichtsphilosophische Thesen," XIV, 1:503.
29. Sholem, *Major Trends in Jewish Mysticism* (1941; New York: Schocken, 1961), p. 17.

saying, interpreting words begins to countervail loss and to orient the desire to redeem that loss. When Celan felt one such word "Close, in the aorta's arch," a meridian was joined. His poem in the fullest sense translates a bright word: "Carried across now, / all the old weeping." Here translation acts not merely to convey or extend but to regenerate tradition: translation and tradition interinanimating, the one action at the heart of the other.

Just what kind of regeneration Paul Celan's poem attests to, whether personal, historical, or spiritual, I do not know. Possibly to Israel's astounding response in June 1967—"Mother Rachel / weeps no more"—though he may have composed this poem before the war itself. Maybe some acute crisis of nervous melancholy had blessedly come "unbinded." Yet isn't it, after all, sheer gratitude simply at meeting up with the Hebrew word, that moves Celan's poem from beginning to end? In translating, I even share that gratitude for a moment, having no way and no need to translate *Ziv*.

THE PROCESS OF TRANSLATION
WILLIAM WEAVER

In the pages that follow I have tried to fix on paper the stages of
an elusive process: the translation of an Italian text into English.
For the operation I have chosen also an elusive author, Carlo Emilio Gadda, partly because his work is not well known to English-
language readers, but mostly because he is an author I am particularly fond of and enjoy translating. I have settled on the first paragraph of "Notte di luna," the opening chapter (or story, as Gadda
would have us believe) in the volume *L'Adalgisa*, originally published in 1944. I have used the Einaudi edition of 1963.

I need hardly say that the description that follows is partial,
perhaps even somewhat misleading, because I have tried to make
conscious and logical something that is, most of the time, unconscious, instinctive. Faced with a choice between "perhaps" and
"maybe," the translator does not put the words on trial and engage
attorneys to defend and accuse. Most probably, he hears the words
in some corner of his mind, and likes the sound of one better than
the other. Of course, his decision is only apparently instinctive. His
instinct will be guided by his knowledge of the author's work, by
his reading in the period. It will almost certainly not be guided by
any rules, even self-made ones. On Thursday, translating Moravia,
he may write "maybe," and on Friday, translating Manzoni, he may
write "perhaps."

Because there are no rules, no laws, there cannot be an absolute
right or an absolute wrong. There can be errors (and even the most
experienced translator has an occasional mishap); there can be
lapses in tone. The worst mistake a translator can commit is to
reassure himself by saying, "that's what it says in the original," and
renouncing the struggle to do his best. The words of the original
are only the starting point; a translator must do more than convey
information (a literary translator, that is).

If someone asks me how I translate, I am hard put to find an
answer. I can describe the physical process: I make a very rapid first
draft, put it aside for a while, then go over it at a painfully slow

William Weaver is the author of several books about opera and a translator of modern Italian literature. He has translated works by Italo Calvino, Alberto Moravia,
Carlo Emilio Gadda, Primo Levi, Pier Paolo Pasolini, and Umberto Eco.

pace, pencil—and eraser—in hand. But that is all outside. Inside, the job is infinitely complex, and what's more, it varies from one author to another. I wish I could describe the thrilling tingle I feel when something seems, finally, to have come right. I prefer not to dwell on the sinking sensation felt when it is obvious that something is dreadfully wrong.

Here, in Italian, is the Gadda paragraph:

> Un'idea, un'idea non sovviene, alla fatica de' cantieri, mentre i sibilanti congegni degli atti trasformano in cose le cose e il lavoro è pieno di sudore e di polvere. Poi ori lontanissimi e uno zaffiro, nel cielo: come cigli, a tremare sopra misericorde sguardo. Quello che, se poseremo, ancora vigilerà. I battiti della vita sembra che uno sgomento li travolga come in una corsa precípite. Ci ha detersi la carità della sera: e dove alcuno aspetta moviamo: perché nostra ventura abbia corso, e nessuno la impedirà. Perché poi avremo a riposare.

And here (without any subsequent cosmesis) is the absolutely first draft of the translation, complete with doubts, alternative solutions, puzzlements. This is the raw material:

> An idea, an idea does not (recall/sustain/aid/repair, in the labor of the building sites, as the hissing devices/machinery of actions transform things into things and the(?) labor/toil is full of sweat and dust. Then distant gold(s) and a sapphire, in the sky: like lashes, trembling above compassionate/merciful/charitable gaze. Which, if we cast it, will still keep watch/be wakeful/alert. The pulses/throbbing of life, it seems, can be overwhelmed/swept away by an alarm, as if in a (precipitous race/dash. The charity of the evening has cleansed us (We are cleansed by the . . . : and where someone is waiting, we move: so that our fate/lot may proceed, and no one will block/impede/hinder it. Because then/afterwards/later we will rest/be able to rest/have our rest."

First thoughts: the passage contains several words I hate. *Cantiere* has to be translated "work site," I suppose, but the Italian word is simpler and more commonplace. Sometimes I translate *cantiere* simply as "job" (cf. *al cantiere* or *in cantiere* can be rendered "on the job"). But I don't think that will work in this case, also because I may have to use "job" immediately afterwards for *il lavoro. Sguardo.* Again, the almost obligatory translation is "gaze." But "gaze" is much more highfalutin than *sguardo,* which could also be "look." But "look," in English, is too vague, can mean too many things. *Dacci uno sguardo* can be "take a look," but *sguardo*, when it is more isolated—as here—probably has to be "gaze." Another word that always seems to cause me problems is *sgomento*. As an adjective, it can sometimes be "aghast." But here it is a noun. "Alarm" does not satisfy me.

Gadda has appended two notes to this first paragraph. As usual, they do not explain much, but rather extend the sentence he is annotating. Here he is concerned that the *alcuno* remain sexually ambiguous. "Someone" will probably do perfectly well. Similarly, he glosses the *nessuno* in the same sentence: it refers to fathers, police, firemen—those who can enforce prohibitions. And he lists, among these, the governor of Maracaibo and tells of a youth who, flouting a veto, tore up his sheets, tied them to make a rope, and escaped from his room, to go off and join Garibaldi.

Notes to myself: avoid ironing out the rhythm, making the sentence structure more normal or conventional; do not try to clarify the meaning when Gadda has deliberately made it murky (translation is not exegesis); try to maintain Gadda's balance between ordinary words (*sudore, lavoro*, etc.) and more exotic words (*zaffiro, detersi*). Find a suitably poetic and cadenced solution to the final, short sentence of the paragraph.

Now a second draft: In the opening sentence, how to capture the force and poetry of the initial repetition? Literally translated ("An idea, an idea . . ."), it sounds wrong to me. How about shifting the negative from the verb to the subject? "No idea, no idea . . ."? Here the repetition sounds even worse. But perhaps, instead of repeating, I should simply enforce the noun. "No idea at all . . ." "Not the least idea . . ." "No, no idea. . . ."

I like this last solution best, because it allows a repetition, even if not the same repetition as Gadda's. It is not the perfect solution, but in translating—and especially in translating Gadda—there are no perfect solutions. You simply do your best.

Sovviene means something like "come to the aid of." In my rapid first draft I even put down "recall," because it can also have the meaning and, when reflexive, can mean "remember." But here it is the verb related to "subvention," not to "souvenir."

Fatica: "effort," but also "toil, labor." There must be a sense of expenditure of strength, a physical effort. *Atti* is more "deeds" than "actions." One of Gadda's quirkish choices (rather than *azioni*).

Now try the first sentence. "No, no idea brings relief to the

labor of the work sites, as the sibilant instruments of action trans-
form things into other things, and the job is full of sweat and dust."
Sibilanti means "hissing," but I have rejected this in favor of
"sibilant," as more Gaddian. It almost suggests speech. And after
first translating *congegni* as "machinery," avoiding the dictionary
translation ("devices," "apparatuses") I settle on "instruments,"
which seems to have more resonance. But then I omit the plural of
atti. Why? It is hard to explain, but partly because I dislike two
plurals in a row, and "instruments" has to remain plural. I have also
added the word "other." Is this exegesis? I hope not. The more
literal first translation sounds gibberish-y.

Next sentence. Another problem of plural. *Ori*. This is common Italian usage, often meaning something like "jewelry" or
"treasure." The successful show of Scythian gold was called in Italy,
Gli ori degli sciti, I believe. A husband will jokingly refer to his
wife's jewelry as her *ori*. But this will not work in English, will it?
We use the plural only in discussing painting ("the reds and golds
in Beato Angelico"), if then.

Other solution: add something like "streaks." "Streaks of gold"
retains the plural; but no, too banal. But perhaps the *uno* before
"sapphire" could be translated as "one," instead of being an indefinite article. *Uno/a* is often a problem in this sense. I'll try it: it may
give the sentence a boost.

"Then distant gold and one sapphire, in the sky: like lashes
quivering above a compassionate glance."

I discard the more literal "trembling," in favor of the less vio-
lent "quivering." And I decide on "compassionate" rather than
"merciful," which, for me, is somehow too physical (perhaps I am
influenced by my memory of the Corporal Works of Mercy, which
I had to learn by heart in the second grade). "Charitable" will not
do, because we have "charity" two sentences later.

Quello, beginning the next sentence, can be troublesome. In
English we don't like to begin sentences with a relative pronoun.
Here the *poseremo* (of which *sguardo* is the object, and to which
quello refers) is a pre-echo of the final word of the paragraph, *riposare*. This assonance will almost surely be lost in English.

Third sentence, then: "The one which, if we cast it, will still
remain vigilant."

In the end I decided that *Quello che* has to be "The one which"
or "That one which." I hate "cast" for *posare*, but what can I do? In
English we cast a glance; the Italians "set" a glance. I decided, too,

that the verb *vigilare* was best turned into a predicate and adjective. But, in a further revision, I may change my mind.

Battiti is tough. Heartbeats are called *battiti* in Italian, but Gadda obviously wants the word also to suggest the banging and pounding of the work site. "Pounding" will not do, because the "poundings of life" sounds like grievous bodily harm. "Throbbing" and "pulse" or "pulsation" rob the sentence of the work-site echo. The *sembra* is also awkward, coming in the middle of the sentence and rerouting its meaning. In a normal English sentence, the "It seems" would come at the beginning, and the sentence would flow smoothly, if boringly, thereafter.

Here's a stab at the sentence: "The beating of life, it seems, can be swept away by a sudden alarm as if in a headlong dash."

I know, "beating" could raise the same objection as "pounding," but—with luck—it may still suggest heartbeat to the reader, and it retains the sense of work at the site. The "it seems" separated necessarily by commas is a somewhat stronger interruption than the *sembra* in Italian, but I think it can stay. And I had to add "sudden" to "alarm" for *sgomento,* partly because the word "alarm" by itself is weak, and also because it could be mistaken for "alarm signal" or even for the work site's siren. I like "headlong," which gives the sense of speed and confusion. In the Italian, *corsa* ("race" or, here, "dash") pre-echoes *corso* in the next sentence. I cannot think of any way to avoid the loss here.

Next sentence: "The charity of the evening has cleansed us: and we move toward someone waiting, that our future may take its course, and no one shall hinder it."

In the first part of the sentence, I reject, of course, the passive. After the colon, I have to shift the Italian word order. "Toward someone waiting we move" sounds poetical in the bad sense. *Ventura* is another word I prefer not to encounter. It means "fortune," in the sense of "soldier of fortune" (*soldato di ventura*), or good luck (*sventura* is "bad luck"). But "fortune" seems too ambiguous in English, and "destiny" or "fate" or even "lot" would be too pretentious and perhaps also too specific.

The meaning of the final sentence is easy enough to understand. It is, more or less: "Because we will later be able to rest." But in the Italian it has an almost biblical ring, and the trick is to exalt the sentence without losing its simplicity, without making it pompous.

I will use the conjunction "for" instead of "because." It has, I believe, a King James version sound. I am tempted to use "shall find rest" or something of the sort, but then I decide it is too risky, too obvious a reference to the Beatitudes. In the end, perhaps simplicity is the best course, as it so often is.

I would say then: "For afterwards we can rest."

One bad loss here: the future tense of *avremo*. But "we shall rest" has a tinge of pompousness.

Now let's put all the sentences together:

> No, no idea brings relief to the labor of the work sites, as the sibilant instruments of action transform things into other things, and the toil is full of sweat and dirt. Then distant gold and a sapphire, in the sky: like lashes quivering above a compassionate glance. The glance which, if we cast it, will remain watchful. The beat of life, it seems, can be swept away by a shock, as if in a headlong dash. The charity of the evening has cleansed us: and we move toward the place where someone is waiting, that our future may unfold, and no one shall hinder it. For afterwards we can rest.

In copying out the separate sentences and combining them, I make some little changes. I decide that "toil" is better than "job," which can suggest more "task." I decide against "one" sapphire, after all; and prefer "watchful" to "vigilant" (too close to the Italian, a *faux ami?*). As I write out "beating," I realize that "beat" conveys the same meaning(s), and I can avoid the -ing, of which there are probably too many in this passage. "Shock" seems to do the work of "sudden alarm" and spares me the adjective. I amplify the *dove alcuno aspetta* clause: a little swell is permissible here, before the almost curt conclusion. Anyway, I have also condensed the clause by using "unfold" for "take its course."

Is that it? Is the translation finished? No. For most of my translating life, I have worked with living authors, and, at this stage, I would probably take my problems to their source, for further discussion, enlightenment, and—afterwards—revision. When I translated Gadda's novels *That Awful Mess on Via Merulana* and *Acquainted with Grief,* I would submit queries to him. Often, in his shy, but imposing manner, he would dismiss the problem, saying simply "cut that." Instead of obeying him, I would approach the tricky passage by another route, taking it up with Gadda's younger friend, the scholar GianCarlo Roscioni, who could almost always either offer the solution himself and, frequently, overcome Gadda's prickly reluctance to reveal his meanings.

Gadda died some years ago; but, happily, I can consult Roscioni. I send him my paragraph, with the pages above; he answers by return mail and, as usual, comes to my aid. First he informs me—what I should have known—that "Notte di luna" was originally a fragment of an unpublished novel written in 1924 and published posthumously in 1983. Roscioni supplies me with a photocopy of the first version of the difficult paragraph. And it is immediately clear that, in the first sentence, *sovviene* does not have the "subvention" meaning, but is closer to the Latin *subvenit* ("comes up," "appears," "materializes"). Gadda, in Roscioni's opinion—and in mine, now—is saying that no exceptional thought materializes to relieve the labor of the work site.

More important, the pesky verb *posare* ("to cast," as "cast a glance") is, in the original version, *riposare,* and so Gadda is saying that when we rest (or are dead) a gaze keeps watch—the eye of God—from the starred heavens.

Roscioni has some doubt about "shock," which is, he thinks, less subjective than *sgomento.* I will think about that, as I write out yet another "final" version of the paragraph.

> No, no Idea appears, in the labor of the work sites, as the sibilant instruments of action transform things into things, and the toil is full of sweat and dirt. Then a distant gold and sapphire in the sky, like lashes quivering above a compassionate gaze. That, if we are at rest, will remain vigilant. The beat of life, it seems, can be swept away by fright, as if in a headlong race. The charity of the evening has cleansed us: and we have moved toward the place where someone is waiting, so that our future may unfold, and no one shall hinder our lot. For afterwards we can rest.

In the end, I decided against "shock," though I am not entirely happy with "fright." "Sudden fear" would be closer, but wasn't it the title of a Joan Crawford movie? It sounds like one. Roscioni disliked "future" for *ventura,* but again "destiny," "fate," have a pompous ring to me. I have stuck with "future" but added "lot" later, less conspicuously at the end of the sentence.

If I were translating all of *L'Adalgisa* (and how I wish a publisher would give me the job/task/toil/blessing), I would have several further opportunities to study and revise this paragraph. My "fair" copies are never completely free of x'd-out words and pencilled-in emendations; and even on the proofs—braving the publisher's reproaches—I make a few, last-minute changes. Once a translation of mine is published, I never re-read it. I know that, if I did, I would soon be reaching for a pencil, to make further additions and subtractions, in the futile pursuit of a nonexistent perfection.

ON TRANSLATING GÜNTER EICH'S POEM "RYOANJI"

CHRISTOPHER MIDDLETON

I have resisted an impulse to write this essay for some time. My
resistance was compounded of doubt and diffidence. To start with,
the translation in question was done to help a student in a German
poetry seminar who knew far less German than the other students;
that specific purpose imposed certain restraints. Even then, my
general rule for translating poems is a rule that is as restraining as
it is naive and absurd: I ask myself if, on reading my translation,
the poet would be able to identify it as his own work, had he now
been writing in English. Next, I doubted whether there was anything I could say that might hold some interest, or even be remotely useful in the vexed realm of verse translation. The diffidence
arose, I expect, from two sources. First, I regard this translation as
a makeshift effort; second, my view of the "meaning" of the original, or rather, perhaps, of what the original signifies in the context
of a certain lyrical canon, remains conjectural, and much still has
to be worked out (often the case with views that derive from translating).

Translation does involve interpretation; misreading, in a nar-
row or broad sense, is usually what upsets a translation. Yet the
two procedures can be incongruous. Why should that be so? If the
original ventured upon is more than usually cryptic, more than
elusively subtle, either procedure is apt to be subverted by the very
capricious edginess of judgment that the original, being so cryptic
or subtle, tends to occasion. This edginess also can tempt the translator to overexplicate. Günter Eich's "Ryoanji" is, in addition, a
text of which the discreet charm consists partly in its seeming, like

Christopher Middleton is professor of Germanic languages and literature at the
University of Texas at Austin. He is widely known as a poet and as a translator of
Goethe, Nietzsche, Trakl, Robert Walser, Gottfried Benn, Paul Celan, Eduard Mo-
rike, and Gerd Hofmann among others.

"Ryoanji," by Günther Eich, is quoted by permission from *Anlässe und Stein-
gärten*, ©Suhrkamp Verlag, Frankfurt-am-Main, 1966.

other late poems of his, to unsay as much as it says. Not that he invented, with defiance or even malice, a type of lyric "utterance" that persistently crushes semantic norms without any recourse to adventurous diction—though that is part of the story. The problem is that his militant skepticism about the value of any individual lyric voice that pretends to speak in an age (or perennial world) of in-authentic (because manipulated) language, of jargons, calques, clichés, and charades of metaphor, is carried in "Ryoanji" to a fairly bleak extreme. Yes, he does say something here, but the poem de-velops only to verge on recanting much of what is said. It builds up its energy by stalling its own emergence, I think. The "mean-ing" that you "carry away" is hardly more weighty than one tuft of dandelion seeds that has landed on your forearm during a walk through a field when all the silver dandelion spheres are being popped and diffused by a fierce breeze. Fair enough. But this kind of semantic glide, in which no signs hold still, in which direct "meanings" are being twitted or deflected, and in which few codes configure as consecutive discourse, does nag a translator, or intox-icate him. Perish the thought that doctrinaires of untranslatability might so much as point to such a glowing *sotto voce* poem as grist for their gloomy mill.

The title matters. Ryoanji is ascertainably a place in Japan, where there are temples and clinics (one of the latter evidently for patients with lung disease). Not a spa exactly—perhaps more like ancient Epidauros. The poem comes out of this milieu and makes little of guidebook details. After several readings, then, I found myself picking up those details that are salient in the poem's glide. This is putting it rather crudely. To be more precise, certain partic-ulars, sensuous ones, became salient in the field of my attention. Then these formed a fluid net of associable sensuous particulars through which the discourse moved. Even that is not quite it. A better figure might be that of a constellation of particulars that rotated in the sky of the discourse. Salient and associable particu-lars, dispersed through the discourse, began to light up and form relatively constant kinships.

Various local features are glimpsed: cameras (toted by tour-ists?), exercises prescribed by physicians with English surnames. Possibly notices are pinned to the walls (messages?), but these are called *Sprachtheorien,* "language theories." Certainly to the river or stream Kamo messages folded as paper boats might be entrusted. Also there are walkways of wood, and there are sandals, which provoke reference to toes. Then there is the coughing, and there is sputum. A voice mutters to itself, the speaker is no less concerned to send messages to friends than other visitors to the place would be. The allusion to smoke signals, with which the poem begins, modulating from the "white" answer to the "black" that is "missed" twenty lines into the poem, might suggest that the speaker is or was a smoker, who once enjoyed a friendly smoke, but who is now concerned with the "fire." "White" / "black" and "smoke" / "fire" are more or less evident contrasts. Generally contrast-in-kinship seems to be the law that regulates the glide of associations (rather than direct argument) organizing the discourse. Accordingly, the translator's first task is to place contrastive words in telling (but still discreet) positions within the phrase or sentence. The contrastive effect has to be subordinated to the glide effect, since it is the latter that probably determines the whole movement of the poem. Contrasts must not be so frontal as to obstruct the glide. Whatever the anxious interpreter of the poem may do to plot the glide as a whole and feel out the kinship system of particulars, the translator ought to resist any impulse to shout (explicate) what the voice has chosen to mutter (implicate). So what will really matter is simply word order.

Rauchzeichen für Freunde,
ein günstiger Tag, windstill,
am Abhang, nordöstlich
antwortet es mir weiß.
Ich mische Kiefer ein.
Und nun Wand an Wand
mit Sprachtheorien,
Wand an Wand
hustet mit Goldzähnen meine Traurigkeit,
auf den Holzgängen
Regen und Holzsandalen,
überall ende ich,
sorgenvoll bewegen
meine Zehen im Finstern
das Finstere,
ich bedaure mich,
ich bin nicht einverstanden mit meinen Zehen
nicht einverstanden mit meinem Bedauern,
ich vermisse die Rauchzeichen,
alt, schwarz und zugeneigt.

Jetzt kommen sie nicht mehr,
jetzt ist Nacht
Jetzt kommt das Feuer,

. . . .

Smoke signals for friends,
the day propitious, no wind,
to northeast, on the slope,
there's an answer for me, white.
I mix pine into it, and jawbone.
And now wall to wall
with theories of language,
wall to wall
my misery coughs with gold teeth,
on the walkways of wood
rain and wooden sandals,
I'm coming everywhere to an end,
my careworn toes
move in the dark
the darkness,
I regret myself,
I don't agree with my toes,
don't agree with my regret,
I miss the smoke signals,
old, black, and affectionate.
Now they no longer come,
now it is night,
now comes the fire,

. . . .

   I had difficulty making sense of lines 4 and 5, also of the phrase
"nun Wand an Wand / mit Sprachtheorien," but translated the latter
literally anyway, since there seemed to be no punning, no double
entendre. As for "ich mische Kiefer ein" and the "white" answer, I
reconstructed mentally a scene in which, beyond pines in the
middle distance, the sky far off is white—this white being a response to the "smoke signals" he's sending (in this poem? or having
just mailed some postcards?). This whiteness would be that of a
blank sky (thus even no answer is an answer?), or else this line
marks the moment at which, having wondered whether to send
signals to friends on a day that is propitious because there's no
wind, the answer is an impulse to write on white paper a poem that
would touch on friendship thematically—as indeed this poem
does.

As for line 5, *Kiefer* means "pine tree," but lacking specific gender or number here it might also mean "jawbone." I was inclined to think that a pun occurs here. Thinking of sending signals and resolving to write the poem, the speaker begins to murmur words in response, to "mix" jawbone into the "white" answer. So, after "pine," I hesitantly added "jawbone," which in English is both noun and verb. (Would the *Kiefer* pun be too coarse to be even thinkable to a masterful German poet? I had doubts, but liked the meatiness of the English line.) The *Kiefer*-as-jawbone aspect might, I conjectured, be the first member in a gliding sequence of physiological cognates—flesh-words: "misery coughs with gold teeth," "toes," "sputum," "raw fish," "prickly skin," "breathing exercises," and "snores" (*Schnarchlauten* = "nasals"). At the end of the second paragraph of the poem *Kiefer* returns, but as *die Kiefern*, this time in pots; the plural form with -*n* shows that in this second context only the tree-sense counts. For that reason perhaps there's a clearer hint there of a greenness, which, even in the first context, would be what is associatively "mixed" into the white and which certainly contrasts with the "black" smoke and the dark (or gloomy) ideas of sickness that follow it in paragraph 3.

"Ich mische Kiefer ein," I later reflected, might be one of Eich's deceptively simple lines that seem to wriggle free from literal sense without being "symbolic," and that function in a poem as markers in a dispersed sequence of perceptions. All dispersed sequences configuring in a poem constitute the text as a "trigonometrical point," upon which certain coordinates, such as space, time, and insight into the historical textures of a particular space, a particular time, happen coolly to converge. His mixing "pine" into the "white" here announces his participation, perhaps, in the space-time continuum he beholds out there. The jawbone/*Kiefer* (*Kiefer*, meaning "jawbone" has no nominative plural form with -*n*) would accent the vocal aspect of this participation. Either way, *Kiefer* cryptically, but with a sure touch, offers a nuance of hope (green) that the white (page) of the "answer" as poem might not come to nought.

Hence, I suspected, the next phrase: "And now wall to wall / with theories of language"—no sooner has the poem begun than, from behind it, the theoretical reflection on language as such both propels and suspends the *thematic* advance of the poem. The speaker is walled in, perhaps, or feels that he is, by messages on walls, notices, posters, and the like, which he disembowels, as it were, to find—haruspication is foreshadowed in the earlier phrase "ein günstiger Tag," a *propitious* or *auspicious* day—neither skin nor significant entrails, but *theories* of language.

So the voice proceeds, against obstacles. Stricken by *Sprachbewußtsein* and coughing, it says "I'm coming everywhere to an end." This self-contradictory voice proceeds, although the speaker doesn't agree with himself, with his toes, even with his self-regret (*Bedauern*—he's feeling sorry for himself). Even then, there's a continuum, for the smoke signals are still in mind, and what comes now is the *fire*.

This was the point at which, while translating, I felt quite excited. The fire phrase in my mind found its way back to Hölderlin's invocation, "Jetzt komme, Feuer!"—the opening words of his late canto "Der Ister"—and to Hölderlin's poem "Andenken," which begins with a northeast wind that promises "fiery spirit to the mariners." The northeast direction stands at the beginning of Eich's poem too, with no wind. Hölderlin later asks, "Wo aber sind die Freunde?" ("But where are my friends?"), and this too is a concern of Eich's. Hölderlin ends with a renowned and cryptic statement about what memory does for the past (in Eich "das Geschehene"), what love does to "steady the gaze," and what poets do to establish what endures. I began to think that Eich's poem might be gliding under pressures similar to those that guided Hölderlin. Yet I shelved the thought and went on translating (to see what might come next) down to the passage about "cameras" being "foreign to me," and onward to the "raw fish." Intertextuality would have to wait.

At the "raw fish" juncture an apparently indifferent and suffering Eich avows that old and native Japanese phenomena are more familiar to him than the décor, or the smoke, or the fire. His sickness concentrates his mind on stark essentials; these include perhaps "Old Japanese" howling voices of Noh and Kabuki actors, to which, typically, an allusion (howling) is made only to stop short: the conceivable referent goes unspoken.

As regards translation the next difficulty came with the "uninfluential / oft-sung puddle" at the start of paragraph 5. *Einflußlos* must be a pun: the puddle has no influx, no streams flow into it. But what puddle is this? On what puddle would petitions drift, to anchor and wait for the collapse of the petitioners and for "concluding remarks"? Is *Pfütze* a meiosis for Kamo/Acheron conceived as a lake, rather than river, in the underworld? *Abschließende Vermerke* might very well be an ironic periphrasis for "obituary notices." The antecedent phrase, "many words with and" is a wry reflection on syntax as a sustaining illusion. People keep on speaking but nobody goes on for ever. Paragraph 5 modulates, then, into a muttered *memento mori*, the acceptance of "heart" and of "heart-renders" in paragraph 4. All I could do for *einflußlos* was "uninfluential," which almost misses the one point (stagnant death), while voicing the other one—that people try not to let death influence them or their presumption to continuance reflected in the way they speak. Throughout this passage the wording tends to be two-edged. Razor sharp, but without the least emphasis or pathos, it meets halfway the fact of death.

So far I've discussed wording, but word order was no less important. The lapidary phrasing had to be grappled with: offhand but dignified, singularizing infinitesimals (e.g., the word *und*), hardly ever downbeat, always crisp, however somber or arcane. There's a world of difference between "on the slope, northeast" and "to northeast, on the slope," between "I stop everywhere" and "I'm coming everywhere to an end," between "cameras are not my thing either" and "cameras too are foreign to me," or between "confided to the puddle / often sung of, uninfluential" and "entrusted to the uninfluential / oft-sung puddle." (As regards interpretation, I inferred that cameras are foreign to the speaker because they would take snapshots [fixed] for later viewing, even for nostalgia, whereas the speaker is there immediately, in the poem's glide.) Here then are paragraphs 3 to 6.

bestenfalls und
schlimmstenfalls.
Ich halte nichts vom Feuer,
ich halte nichts vom Rauch
und nichts vom Atem.
Ich halte etwas vom Husten,
vom Auswurf,
von den finsteren Gedanken der Krankheit
vom Finsteren.
Mir sind auch Fotoapparate fremd
und die Kiefern im Blumentopf.
Die Kakifrüchte verstehe ich besser
und das heulende Altjapanisch
und die Verbeugungen am Ende der Rolltreppe
und den rohen Fisch.

Und viele Vokabeln mit und,
und alle

verräterisch herzzerreißend,
ich begrüße dich, Herz,
begrüße die Zerreißenden,
vielleicht gäbe es
Papierschiffe auf dem Kamo,
aus Bittschriften gefaltet,

das wärs,
anvertraut der einflußlosen
viel besungenen Pfütze,
ankern sie und warten
auf den Untergang der Bittsteller
und abschließende Vermerke.

Abends
steigt das Fieber in den Klinikbetten,
manches erfährt man da,
für manches sind die Beweise
nicht gültig,
im Papierkorb
rasseln die welken Blätter,
die Igel unter den Gebüschen,
fast stumm,
wohnen zugänglich
dem Stachelfell meiner Einsichten,
wir reiben sie aneinander,
höchstens Moos wird bewegt,
die Welt nicht.
Wir tauschen die Adressen,
wir tauschen
unsere persönlichen Fürwörter aus,

wir haben vieles gemeinsam,
die Sonnenaufgänge,
die Zukunft bis neunzehnhundertsieben.
Dann üben wir das Atmen,
gemeinsam,
nach den Vorschriften von Cheyne
und den Vorschriften von Stokes,
so bringen wir die Zeit leicht hin
mit den Schnarchlauten
unsrer innersten Gedanken.

all being for the best,
all for the worst.

I think nothing of the fire,
I think nothing of the smoke
and nothing of my breath.
I think something of coughing,
of sputum,
of the dark ideas of sickness,
of the darkness.
Cameras too are foreign to me,
so are the pine trees in flower pots.
I understand the kaki fruit better
and howling Old Japanese,
bowings at the end of the escalator,
and raw fish.

And many words with and,
and all of them
treacherously heartrending,
heart, hallo,
hallo to the renders,
perhaps there'd be
paper boats on the Kamo,
folded petitions,

that would be it,
entrusted to the uninfluential
oft-sung puddle
they anchor and wait
for the petitioners to collapse
and concluding remarks.

Temperatures rise
evenings in the clinic beds,
you learn things there,
the proofs for some of them
are not valid,
wilted leaves rustle
in the waste paper basket,
the hedgehogs under bushes,
almost dumb,
live responsive
to the prickly hide of my insights,
we rub them against one another,
at most moss is moved,
the world is not.
We exchange addresses,

we exchange our
personal recommendations,

we have much in common,
the risings of the sun,
the future up to nineteen seven.
Then we do breathing exercises,
together,
according to the rules of Cheyne
and the rules of Stokes,
so we pass the time away lightly
with the snoring nasals
of our most intimate thoughts.

Smoke—fire—rising temperatures: the gliding sequence of
phrases, which are chords of things thought and things perceived,
has by now arrived at a crossways, from which the sundry themes
branch out anew: the pathology of lung disease, the *Blätter*
("pages," "leaves"), exchange of messages, eventually the lapse into
snores "of our most intimate thoughts." The *Blätter* are both withered leaves and pages crumpled and tossed into the wastepaper
basket—their rustling serves to introduce, by association, the
hedgehogs, which hereafter carry the theme of message and communication, oddly enough. (Hedgehogs in central and northern
Europe forage through leaves on the ground beneath hedges: the
rustling sound betrays their presence.) "Die welken Blätter" I
translated as "wilted leaves," since their presence in the wastepaper
basket would suffice to indicate that pages too are meant (also I
wondered if oracular leaves were implied). Here the sequel called
for desperately literal translation. The gist is that written messages
might as well be for the hedgehogs, communication with fellow
humans being barely thinkable. It even seems that Eich did his
breathing exercises in company with hedgehogs. Generally, paragraph 6 moves toward a vanishing point. Confidence in self and
respondent, contact between sender and message even, perish, dis-
solved into the sound of leaves withered, pages rustling, and
snores. Yet the poem does continue. Certain phrases—"insights,"
"exchange," "the risings of the sun," "the future," "together," "intimate thoughts"—are members of a brighter contrapuntal series.
Sustained by its own oscillation, the discourse quietly negates the
very theme it modulates. A characteristically skewed drift develops
in these lines, barely "coherent" as they must seem to be if controlled argument is what a reader had expected. "The future up to

nineteen seven" is, however, in the context of the poem's whole trigonometry, no less concrete than "risings of the sun" or the rules of Cheyne and of Stokes: the phrase comes apparently out of the blue, and then its import seems to have no sequel. Yet its sequel comes, at the end of paragraph 8: "Where in baskets, sacks, tubs / past event piles up"—Eich was born in 1907, but at the time of writing he knows he'll soon be dying; thus, in a sense, the phrase "the future up to nineteen seven" implies a pre-existence in which he might, just as well as now, have hobnobbed with hedgehogs. The phrase thus opens a bracket around his lifetime. The bracket is *not* closed, to the extent that, against all odds, the poem continues into its fullest paradoxical insight six lines from the end—"Unser Ort ist im freien Fall" ("Our *dwelling* is in *free fall*"; my italics).

The eighth paragraph moves toward a more affirmative note, but hardly strikes one. The everyday visible and speakable world is left for others, while "we"—hedgehogs in their signification here, at least, also poets and friends—are an ongoing conspiracy. "Clan" in German has the sense of a conspiratorial group or secret cabal. I could not find an English term to match the complexion of these senses in German. "Cabal" might have done, but it's too resonant, too abstruse, lexically speaking, for this context. The translation of "im zugespitzten Augenblick" as "at the critical moment" lacks the hedgehog innuendo (*Spitze* = "point," as hedgehog spines are pointy), but it sustains the notion of poetic time, the time of and in the poem, as a time in which language is critical in every sense (a notion that Eich developed in his Büchner Prize address of 1960). The past is not renounced; "we" just don't listen to it, falling as we do, living in bushes, darknesses, and clinic beds. Finally "we" do also have something to impart: the hedgehog words (prickly, secret, resistant), and "we" do stand by something—*Unordnung*, "misrule" (last paragraph).

Here "wir halten auf Unordnung" is a wry grammatical twist. The normal expectation of a predicate after the rigorous "wir halten auf" would be of something steady, like order, law, or principle. I'm not sure if "we abide by misrule" captures this air of paradox; perhaps "abide" stands also too close to "dwelling" and so impedes the glide effect. Paragraphs 8 and 9 run as follows.

Wenn einer will,
soll er Fotos in die Schaukästen hängen,
Anekdoten erzählen
oder welchen zuhören,

die Lage besprechen,
Ornithologie, Schönschreiben,
vor allem Gute Nacht.
Ein entschlossener Clan, verharren wir
mit unsern Igeln
im zugespitzten Augenblick,
drehen uns nicht mehr um,
wo in Körben, Säcken, Fässern
das Geschehene sich stapelt,

ein Lagerhaus, offen für jeden,
da schlagen die Türen, schallen Schritte,
wir horchen nicht hin, sind auch taub,
unser Ort ist im freien Fall.
Büsche, Finsternisse und Klinikbetten,
wir siedeln uns nicht mehr an,
wir lehren unsere Töchter und Söhne die Igelwörter
und halten auf Unordnung,
unseren Freunden mißlingt die Welt.

Anyone wanting to,
let him hang photos in the display cases,
tell anecdotes
or listen to some,
discuss the situation,
ornithology, calligraphy,
Good Night above all.
We persist, a resolute clan,
with our hedgehogs
at the crucial moment,
for us there's no turning back now
to where, in baskets, sacks, tubs
past event piles up,

a storehouse, open to anyone,
doors slam, footsteps ring,
we don't hearken, we're deaf, too,
our dwelling is in free fall.
Bushes, darknesses and clinic beds,
now we never settle down,
we teach our daughters and our sons
the hedgehog words
and we abide by misrule,
the world does not work out
for friends of ours.

The last line epitomizes the contrastive glide of associative sequences (or "chords") and it is also a grammatical paradox. Most of my versions of it were fumingly deleted. They indicated something that the German does not, namely, that the "world" is a washout for our friends. This could only imply that "our friends" are disdainful of the world, that the world is at fault. In fact you can say in German, *es mißlingt mir, es ist mir mißlungen,* but more commonly the phrase is followed by an infinitive construction, or else it follows wording that indicates what you have failed to do. It is quite idiosyncratic to say that the world (not just a neutral "it") *mißlingt* for somebody. And if you translate the phrase colloquially as "our friends are losers in this world," then "this world" hints at the existence of another (no such hint in Eich). Even "in the world" would make the phrase so limp as to be contrary to the whole tenor of the poem. The sense is that friends of ours are misfits and the world goes wrong *for them,* insofar as they are not, in the world, achievers. The problem was to find wording that had some finality (for the closure) and yet was as light as it was precise. The best I could do was to switch the word order and include two inconspicuous alliterations, so that, phonically at least, an air of provisional finality rather than resounding closure could be captured. Thus— "the world does not work out / for friends of ours."

While translating the poem, I became more and more intrigued by the thought that it might be a complicated, but really quite breezy, counterpart to Hölderlin's poem "Andenken" (1802–3). There are parallels: fire, a foreign scene, a deepening meditation, absent friends, a quest, an affirmation of poetry, a wondering about memory as divination of structures in time. (In a previous essay I proposed that Hölderlin's poem pioneers a concept of *mémoire involontaire*.)[1] "Andenken," too, is a poem that glides associatively rather than progressing steadily from stage to stage in a deliberate way and with a deliberate argument—it improvises. However, I soon came to think that "Ryoanji" must be a transposition, rather than a counterpart, and that, vast and intricate as a poet's memory may be, its behavior can be capricious. I doubted that Eich would have sat down deliberately to write a critique, parody, or revision of "Andenken."

More likely, "Andenken" was for Eich a memory trace. The text

---

1. Christopher Middleton, "Syntax and Signification in Hölderlin's 'Andenken,'" *The Pursuit of the Kingfisher* (Manchester and New York: Carcanet Press, 1983).

of it, stripped down to the status of a ghostly paradigm, was not so much a skeleton in Eich's memory closet as a voice murmuring from the Great Memory. If he had been fully and frontally conscious of it as an antecedent, he might have been frustrated by its presence. After all, the free movement of a poet's imagination depends not least on what he has forgotten. What a poet forgets, how he forgets, and how he regenerates what he has forgotten, are matters just as important as his contests with events and texts remembered. My ideas on this score were supported by one other instance of Eich's forgetting that I discovered twenty years ago, and that has not, I believe, received any attention. In 1945 Eich wrote a poem that is very famous and yet, for all its independent merit as a text marking a historic situation, echoes an earlier poem, as regards its grammar, so closely as to be a sort of subtle transformation of the earlier poem's form. Eich's "Inventur" of 1945 seems to have arisen from a memory, more or less submerged, of Richard Weiner's poem "Jean Baptiste Chardin."[2] Weiner's poem, which is spoken by the eighteenth-century painter of still lifes, appeared in a German translation in 1916, in *Jüngste tschechische Lyrik,* a little anthology published in Berlin by Verlag Der Aktion.[3] The odds are that Eich would have known this collection when he was studying Chinese art in Berlin during the later 1930s. Richard Weiner's poem (11 quatrains) begins as follows:

To je můj stůl,
to jsou mé papuče,
to je má sklenice,
to je můj čajník.

To je můj etažer,
to moje dýmka,
to je má cukřenka,
rodinný odkaz . . .

---

2. Richard Weiner, *Usmevave Odrikam* (Prague, no date, privately printed). The copy I saw was in the possession of Karel Teige in 1917.

3. *Jüngste tschechische Lyrik: Eine Anthologie* (Berlin-Wilmersdorf: Verlag der Wochenschrift *Die Aktion,* 1916). The German text of Richard Weiner's "Jean Baptiste Chardin" follows:

Dies ist mein Tisch,   Dies meine Etagere,
Dies meine Hausschuh,   Dies meine Pfeife,
Dies ist mein Glas,   Dose für Zucker,
Dies ist mein Kännchen.   Großvaters Erbstück.

This is my table,
these are my slippers,
this is my glass,
this is my tea-maker.

These are my shelves,
this is my pipe,
this is my sugar bowl,
this is my heirloom . . .

and so on, observing the same simplicity throughout, ending

To je má žena.
To je můj obraz.

This is my wife.
This is my painting.

Eich's "Inventur" (7 quatrains) begins as follows:

Dies ist meine Mütze,
dies ist mein Mantel,
hier mein Rasierzeug
im Beutel aus Leinen.

Dies ist mein Eßzimmer,
Dies meine Ecke,
Dies ist mein Hund,
Dies meine Katze.

Hier ist mein Wedgewood,
Dort ist mein Sevrès.
Das lustige Bildchen,
Fragos Geschenk.

Bläuliche Schalen
Hab' ich sehr gern.
Blumen im Fenster
Liebe ich sehr.

Fuchsien aber
Seh ich am liebsten.
Meine Charlotte
Liebet den Flieder.

Täglich um elfe
Frühstücken wir.

Abends um achte
Deckt man zu Tisch.

Esse am liebsten
Spargel mit Sauce,
Wildpret auf Pfeffer,
Erdbeer mit Creme.

Und die Charlotte
Liebt ihre Austern,
Hühnchen auf Schwammerln,
Hummerragout.

Gut ist's zu Hause,
Sehr gut zu Hause.
Dies meine Ecke,
Dies meine Hausschuh.

Glattes Email
Glanzüberquillt.
Dies ist mein Weib.
Dies ist mein Bild.

Konservenbüchse:
Mein Teller, mein Becher,
ich hab in das Weißblech
den Namen geritzt . . .

This is my cap,
this is my coat,
this here is my razor
in a bag made of linen.

Tin can:
my dish, my cup,
into the metal
I've scratched my name . . .

and so on, varying the grammar as he presents the minimal cosmos
of the poet as prisoner-of-war, and ending nevertheless

Dies ist mein Notizbuch,
dies meine Zeltbahn,
dies ist mein Handtuch,
dies ist mein Zwirn.

This is my notebook,
this is my tarpaulin,
this is my towel,
this is my thread.

The question remains: If I had only read and reread "Ryoanji,"
would I have detected its affinity to "Andenken"? Or another question arises: Was I so spellbound by translating as a mimetic act that
I was susceptible to an illusion that "Ryoanji" bore an affinity to
"Andenken"? There's no way to answer either question. I had
known the poem for two years before I set about trying to translate
it, and I no longer recall at which precise stage the Hölderlin text
began to impinge on my response to the fire detail in Eich's poem.
Yet I do suspect that attempts to fathom the gist of Eich's cryptic
phrasing, and to grasp links between his gliding sequenced chords
of detail in order to translate with fidelity, gave my memory the
time and steadied my attention enough to allow me to perceive,
clearly, across all disparities, the terms of a conversation, as it were,
between "Ryoanji" and "Andenken," a conspiratorial dialogue.
Certainly Hölderlin belongs to what Eich calls the "resolute clan"

of poets whose voices call across epochs to one another, if to nobody else.

Viewing the whole situation thus far, as regards interpreting
and translating this poem, I began to cast about for a paradigm in
which to frame my experience of it, possibly to frame experience
of cryptic poems in any language you know only from the outside.
First I thought of Michel Leiris and his anthropological theory of
topsy-turvy or scrambled language.[4] In that theory certain kinds of
topsy-turvy utterance (like Eich's hedgehogs) might provide (for
"primitive" as well as "sophisticated" people) a contact with spirits
and the dead. Leiris writes of ceremonies that involve "a language
of the other side . . . a disjointed, dislocated, danced rather than
devoutly dressed-up discourse" by which "the horror of future an-
nihilation, still noxious but now more diffused, is drawn out of its
diabolically imperceptible nullity thanks to the illusion of a bridge
linguistically suspended." These words reminded me that since
1945 a number of German poets have been revising the Orphic
code by cultivating a countersensical lyric idiom—Nelly Sachs,
Paul Celan, sometimes Johannes Bobrowski, nowadays Oskar Pas-
tior, and, in his peculiar way, also Ernst Jandl.

But a more suitable paradigm, no less extreme, I find in the
short chapter called "The Priest on the Wall" in Colette's book, *My
Mother's House*.[5] Not quite eight years old, Colette picked up the
French word for "presbytery"—*presbytère*. Its meaning was unknown to her, and she felt "enriched by a secret and a doubt," because this word had so intrigued her with its mystery and "with its
harsh and spiky beginning and the brisk trot of its final syllables."
First she used it privately to designate anything or anyone worthy
of a malediction. Later on, she writes, "I began to suspect that
'presbytery' might very possibly be the scientific term for a certain
little yellow-and-black striped snail." I wonder if I got any further
than that stage in attempting to translate "Ryoanji."

4. Michel Leiris, *Langage tangage* (Paris: Ed. Gallimard, 1985). The passage
cited in James Clifford's translation appeared in *Sulfur*, no. 15 (1986): 35–36.
5. Colette, *My Mother's House and Sido* (New York: Farrar, Straus, & Giroux,
1953; seventh printing 1981), pp. 30–32.

ON TRYING TO TRANSLATE JAPANESE
Edward Seidensticker

First, something on literal translation. One cannot be enthusiastic about the results thus far of literal translation from the Japanese. It has been responsible for the "by your honorable shadow" school and for that quaint procession of Orientals led by Mr. Moto. Still, it would be hard to deny that something like the literal note can be caught for brief, inspired flights:[1]

> When the newspaper announcing the emperor's death arrived, my father said: "Oh! Oh!" And then, "Oh, His Majesty is gone at last. I too. . . ." My father then fell silent.

> When the door had closed behind him, Mikuni said, spitting out the words, "There's a fine guy for you. That damned Official Business has gotten scared. 'Use whatever translation fits the context.' That's a fine business. What nonsense!"

> "Wait! That won't do!" called Tojiro, throwing his arms around the young man to stop him, and he called for help to people living near the shrine. "Hey, there, Yu San of the Hashimotoya, hey there, come on over. Hey, there, Matsu no Ji of the Shintaku, come and help me!"

> All I could say was, "Oh, Oh!"
> At cherry-blossomed Yoshino.

But the pitch cannot be maintained for long. Most translators will decide, after the oh's and the ah's, after the blubbering that never seems to strike the Japanese as sentimental, and therefore presumably isn't, that something must be done.

The literalist, who insists that every word in the original must show in the translation, has his place, no doubt, in translation for specialists. One does not wish to dismiss him. He faces puns and honorifics with grim determination, he annotates as he translates,

Edward Seidensticker has written extensively on intercultural understanding between the United States and Japan. He is the translator of *The Tale of Genji* (1976).

1. The first three quotations are from published translations of Japanese fiction. The fourth is a poem. Two of the translators are American, one is an Englishman, and one is a Japanese.

he spares himself none of the problems—except the problem of what is to be done about the literary quality of the original.

To the nonliteralist, uneasy lest there be something more important than puns and honorifics in his original, the real difficulties begin here. What, in fact, is to be done? Writing in 1791, Lord Woodhouselee found an answer. Unfortunately, it is an answer that rather contradicts itself. "The style and manner in a Translation should be of the same character with that of the Original." In other words, it should have the spirit of the foreign language. "A Translation should have all the ease of original composition." In other words, it should have the spirit of English. Even between two languages as near as German and English, Woodhouselee is asking for a miracle. Can a philosopher simultaneously sound like Kant and William James?

And the farther apart the languages, the more real the contradiction. Without knowing a word of Russian, one senses that Constance Garnett's "style and manner" are not those of her Russians. How else explain the fact that her Tolstoy and Turgenev and Dostoyevski all sound exactly alike? One cannot believe that three such disparate geniuses sound alike in Russian. And when she offers Russianisms, "little mother" and the like, one feels that she is not quite in English. Sometimes she has chosen one of Woodhouselee's principles, sometimes the other, and so to a degree have all translators. Ezra Pound too has made his choice, and incidentally dismissed Woodhouselee's other principle, that the translator must convey the *meaning* of the original.

Japanese and English are very different languages. An English sentence hastens to the main point and for the most part lets the qualifications follow after. A Japanese sentence prefers to keep one guessing. The last element in the sentence reveals whether it is positive or negative, declaratory or interrogative. "I do not think that . . ." begins an English sentence; ". . . this I do not think" ends a Japanese sentence, having coyly held off the fact of belief or disbelief to the end.

There is a rather tentative air about Japanese that disappears when the sentence is put into even "literal" English. It tends to disappear too in Japanese, and to take with it the last vestiges of sentence structure, when circumstances require that one come quickly to the point. Hence the strange nature of Japanese telephone conversations. Every few words the speaker must stop to ask whether he is being followed; and he will repeat until he has been reassured. He must ask because he is dismembering his Japanese sentence as it would be dismembered only in the most surrealist of poetry.

Here is the original order: "The I yesterday to you introduced from Osaka aunt tomorrow afternoon on the Sea Breeze Express is going back."

And over the telephone: "My aunt, yes? The one from Osaka, yes? The one I introduced you to, yes? Well, she's going back, yes? Tomorrow afternoon, yes? On an express, the Sea Breeze."

The Japanese sentence has taken on a certain twentieth-century efficiency by being dismembered and reassembled in something like the English word order. A glance back at the original should suggest something else about Japanese sentences: they manage to get by without certain connectives considered indispensable in English. They have no relative pronouns. Adjectival clauses, however long, must precede their nouns. Sentences therefore have a way of going on forever before they come to a noun, and forever and a day before they come to a main verb.

Japanese gets by without many other things. Grammatically it is one of the world's simplest languages. Nouns are not declined, and are without gender. Verbs are elaborately conjugated in classical Japanese, simply in modern Japanese, but in neither case with specific reference to person or number. Adjectives are very much like verbs—in the absence of relative pronouns, both must directly modify nouns—and are in fact conjugated like verbs, without reference to person or number or to gender. Though modern Japanese has a wide variety of personal pronouns, they are not used as unreservedly as in English—indeed too frequent repetition makes them intrude as English nouns do.

The subtleties of the classical language particularly are thus the work of verbs and adjectives, and a verb is not always adequate, as it would be in Latin, to show whether it is I, you, or he who is doing or is being done by. Nevertheless, subjects are in principle omitted. The deficiency is remedied in part by honorifics. Classical verbs and to a lesser extent modern verbs have delicate honorific variations and are capable of small though not always crystalline distinctions. If I am a prince and you are a middling courtier, the case is simple: the two of us will use entirely different verb forms and even different verbs. If I, a courtier, am talking to you, a prince, of my father, the verb forms become more complex. And when I, a prince, am talking to you, a courtier, of what your father said about my child, toward whom I am inclined to use affectionately exaggerated honorifics—they are indescribable.

In sum, there is an insubstantial, tentative quality about the language. As a literary medium, it has virtues and vices, and both are trials for the translator.

"You didn't!"
"Oh, yes, I did."
"But why?"
"Can't you guess?"

If this is a conversation in English between Maude and George, the properly introduced reader has no trouble following it. But let us imagine that the speakers are respectively Maude, George, Aunt Margaret, and Uncle John. An English writer must come right out and say so. In Japanese, however, a skilful use of verbs, plus an occasional pronoun, can make the conversation quite clear as it stands. It could go on for pages, as even Ivy Compton-Burnett could not, without overt reference to a speaker.

In English it must be:

"You didn't!" said Maude.
"Oh, yes, I did," said George.
"But why?" said Aunt Margaret.
"Can't you guess?" said Uncle John.
"Because I loved her," said George.
"You should have told me," said Aunt Margaret.

It becomes a choice between this monotony and the elegant variation (he replied, she responded, he reflected, she retorted) that so annoyed Fowler in Meredith. Either way, the pace falters, and the reader is soon more interested in the squirming translator than in what is being said.

If, in quick modern Japanese prose, verbs carry much of the burden, in classical prose it is verbs and adjectives that do almost everything. The doer is mentioned as seldom as possible, and then with averted eye, as if the princess's screen had fallen while she was at her toilet. A person of importance is almost never referred to by name. He must be "the Minister from the Horikawa Palace" or "the Counsellor from the Ninth Ward" or simply "the Shining One" or "the Fragrant One."

Lafcadio Hearn killed words like "misty" and "semi-diaphanous" for describing things Japanese, and yet one wants to revive them to describe the prose of the tenth and eleventh centu-

ries. Events which have been like salts in solution somehow become more tangible, assertive, out in the open, by having specific
English nouns assigned as subjects. "Floating prose" might describe the effect of the Japanese and thereby free us from "misty."
Or "foggy prose," perhaps. Certainly a quick shift from the original
Tale of Genji to Dr. Waley's translation can be like the moment in
the movies when the London fog lifts and the adversaries stand
face to face in the gaslight.

Because of Murasaki Shikibu's reluctance to name names, Dr.
Waley is frequently at odds with the Japanese commentators, and
the commentators are frequently at odds with one another. Here,
in Dr. Waley's translation, we find a young man from the capital
peeping in upon two secluded young ladies:

> "How strange!" said the lute-player. "One can beckon to the
> moon with one's plectrum just as one summons people with a fan."
> Her face was raised towards the window while she spoke, and Kaoru
> could see enough of it to reach the conclusion that the speaker was
> decidedly good-looking.
>
> "It was to turn back the setting sun that the plectrum was used.
> Yours is quite a new idea!" The person who said this was propped
> against a cushion, and her head was bowed over a zithern that lay on
> the floor in front of her. She laughed as she spoke, but there was at
> the same time a certain seriousness in her manner of making the cor-
> rection, as though facts were of great importance to her. "Well,
> whether I invented the idea or not," replied the elder girl, "you cannot
> deny that lutes and moons have a great deal to do with one another."

The recent commentators have it the other way: the "lute-
player" is the younger sister, the person propped against the cushion the elder. The surface evidence would seem to be in Dr. Waley's
favor. We have been told some pages before that the older sister
was taught by her father to play "the lute." The second speaker uses
honorifics which more become a younger sister, unless the older is
using them in derision. The commentators, however, feel strong
enough to fly in the face of all this because the disparate natures of
the two girls require it. The elder is melancholy, the younger mildly
frivolous. The possibility that Murasaki may have meant both of
them to be rather more complicated bundles of contradictions is
not admitted.

The speaker at any moment, then, is so uncertainly designated
that the most general of considerations can override the textual

evidence. (Dr. Waley's Kaoru, incidentally, is "the Fragrant One."
He is here known only as "the captain," although the book abounds
in captains.) The difficulty is not that the language has changed.
The standard literary language of a hundred years ago, which can
be read with some ease by educated Japanese, is nearer to the language of Murasaki than modern English is to Chaucer. The difficulty is rather suggested by this question: what would Murasaki
have thought of her own prose if she had been trained in modern
English? (A Japanese novelist once told me that he had not realized
how ambiguous he was until he saw himself in translation.) For all
I know, translators from Latin and Greek may be troubled sometimes to know who is speaking or doing, but the literature on
translation would suggest that the reverse is more often the case.
The translator must work to keep what is almost too lucid in the
original from being merely flat in English. The Greeks and Romans
were sufficiently interested in doers to make quite clear who they
were.

Altogether, there is an indecisiveness about Murasaki and her
Genji, and a sort of vague, generalized mood that comes before
particular emotions. "Out with it, woman, out with it!" one wants
to say to her. But never, mutatis mutandis, to Dr. Waley, who announces his decision even when he has to take chances.

"It was near to the fish-weirs, which rather spoilt the view,"
says Dr. Waley. There is only a general dissatisfaction in Murasaki's
sentence—something about the fish-weirs displeases. Evidence
from other sources would indicate, as a matter of fact, that people
loved the sight of the weirs but hated the sound of them.

Almost always, Dr. Waley's humor is crisper than whatever humor there is in the original. " 'You will be going to the Fishers'
Fête, of course?' everyone said to him. 'No,' said Kaoru. 'I think I
shall manage to keep clear of the *ajiro* ["fish-weirs"], as indeed most
of the fish do.' " There is a pun in the original, which Dr. Waley has
replaced with this pleasantry, but if it is humorous it is humorous
in a wan, self-pitying way, far from Dr. Waley's tart Britishness.

Or here is Dr. Waley in a somewhat longer pleasantry: "Moreover, wherever he went, there hung about him a strange fragrance
which, though it procured for him several gratifying successes, in
the end proved so embarrassing that he did everything he could
think of to get rid of it. 'These Court gentlemen do know how to
make themselves smell!' he said. 'It's beyond me how they get hold
of such scents.' "

Though this is rather near the letter of the original, it is somehow different. Murasaki has since the war been made a sort of
people's heroine by the Japanese Left, but she had her aristocratic
ways. One feels that she would not have understood Dr. Waley's
affectionate amusement at the commoner who briefly smelled like
a courtier.

These examples have taken us some distance from the fact that
Japanese tends to do without names and brought us to another
fact, perhaps a cause of the first, perhaps a result, perhaps another
way of saying the same thing: Murasaki's Japanese is of a world
quite alien to modern English. It is a world of Buddhist evanes-
cence in which a combination of resignation and self-pity seems no
fault. If Mr. Pope's *Iliad* is not Homer, Dr. Waley's *Genji* is frequently not Murasaki. On the whole Dr. Waley seems brisk and
positive because he lives in a brisker world and writes a more positive language.

The *Genji* is robust by comparison with most works of the
period. Here, as literal as I can make it, is the opening sentence of
a famous journal. "Things of this sort are over, the world is uncertain, and there was a person who went through it, neither here nor
there." I would perhaps not now be as exuberantly free as when I
first tried translating it: "The years of my youth have passed, and I
can see little in them that suggests greatness," which dismisses the
cliché in the second clause. Still, the translation seems defensible.
In the same journal there are poems whose puns mean one thing if
the writer is a man and quite another if a woman, but the subject
is of course missing, and the evidence will support either sex.

Dr. Waley could certainly have come nearer literal translation
than he did. Thus he could have evaded the issue by identifying
neither of his two musical sisters and leaving the reader to decide
whether the melancholy sister does have her frisky moments, or the
frisky sister has in the course of time learned to play the lute. Another device would be to avoid subjects—put the whole thing in
the passive. Then no one could accuse the translators of assigning
subjects arbitrarily. Nor would the precise translator have trouble
finding what to do with the Japanese passive: "and thus the thing
of its being done was done," "and thus was accomplished the fact
of the poem's being recited," or something of the sort.

Another solution has been hit upon by the bracket school:
translators under the influence of French Orientalists, who have
out-Germaned the Germans, put in brackets every word which has
no specific sanction in the original and may therefore be considered

an intrusion by the translator. "[George] saw [Maude] to [the] bus stop." No subjects in Japanese? All subjects to the brackets. No articles in Japanese? All articles will be resolutely surrounded. But this is really cheating. The subjects and articles are not rendered invisible by the brackets, and we are no nearer the original by its having become unreadable.

The next centuries saw the rise of a hybrid Sino-Japanese style, in which the flow of Japanese verbs and adjectives is interrupted by rocklike Chinese nouns. Chinese nouns are stubbornly self-reliant and will take part in a sentence only with the greatest reluctance. The effect therefore is as of cold-buttered rum. One has only to note the physical appearance of the sentences to guess what is happening. The Japanese elements move along in dips and bends, the Chinese compounds are large black blocks in their midst. The resources of English typography are not up to imitating the effect, though a little might be done:

"The sound of the bell of the Gion Shoja
     echoes
                    Theimpermanenceofthings.
The color of the blossoms of the sal-tree
     reveals the truth that
                    Allwhoprospermustfall."

This sort of Chinoiserie—fundamentally it is a mechanical attempt to change nounless Japanese into something more Chinese and therefore by definition better—has produced a turn of mind which, one suspects, the Japanese share with the Germans. If you can't think of the answer any other way, make up a new word for it, and no one can possibly challenge you. "No, I meant *timishness,* and I defy you to prove the contrary." Thus the noun, black and menacing, takes on an absolute authority, and the translator who tries his hand at the Not and the Not-not and the Neither-not-nor-not-not knows that before long one Zen scholar or another will be reducing him to a whistle. Zen is an extreme example, but one learns not to be surprised when words in an article for a mass-circulation magazine are not to be found in any dictionary. They seem to make sense until one considers what to do with them in English.

The power of nouns is if anything more oppressive today, when the new word has most likely been "borrowed" not from Chinese but from English. Here, in a recent translation, is a sentence that must have caused the translator pain: "Even if the ideal itself is just a life illusion, we cannot live without it." The words "life illusion" are English in the original. I was once asked, and declined, to translate a symposium which came to the weighty conclusion that literature must have, in English, "origin."

In the late nineteenth century, Japanese prose style was revolutionized. Today it is fairly near the spoken language, though with some tendency toward verb forms not used in ordinary speech. Few of the old problems have been solved, however. When it is most modern, it tends to become translatorese, cluttered with transcendental neo-Chinese nouns. And when it is conservative it still floats along, content far more than any important European language to do without overt actors. Just to show that it could be done, a well-known contemporary author once wrote a short story without a single grammatical subject, and the remarkable thing was that no one noticed.

Another problem in modern Japanese brings us to the ultimate in the untranslatable. Japanese admirers of French or German or English try to rewrite their own language as if it were one or another of them, and thus outrage it to the core. The cramped style that results is an argument against "cultural exchange." It is unlovely in the original, and it quite defies rendition into English. How is one to find an equivalent for a style whose most conspicuous feature is, say, a straining to introduce relative pronouns?

It is not easy to think of similar problems in translating *from* English, but one or two timid little analogies do suggest themselves. Think of trying to translate into French Mark Twain's parody of translation into French, or of trying to find Hebrew equivalents for all the Hebraisms Monsignor Knox found in the Authorized Version. Or think of the twisted sentences that school children have for centuries been required to write because the Romans happened not to (and the French happen not to) end their sentences in prepositions. Must a translator feel responsible for reproducing these last, twistedness and all, in Latin or French? Think of trying to recapture in French the effect of Winston Churchill's reply to cavillers about final prepositions.

Woodhouselee had an answer. "The style and manner in a Translation should be of the same character with that of the Original," but if an author is sometimes uneasy, change him. If Homer is occasionally beneath himself, bring him back up again. Woodhouselee lived in a day when important authors wrote well. In a day when many do not, the translator seems to be allowed less freedom by the critics. Dreiser is ungainly in English. Very well, the translator has his choice: leave Dreiser alone or put him into ungainly French or Russian.

If Dreiser's trouble was deafness, the trouble of the modern Japanese writer is the reverse. His ungainliness comes from too lively a sensitivity to English or French grace. The translator might conceivably, miraculously, find an English equivalent for a tense Japanese imitation of a tranquil English relative pronoun, but no one would understand. "The translation is adequate though a trifle plodding," the *Times Literary Supplement* would say.

To reproduce something like the effect, one might try the opposite: leave out all relative pronouns. But then the *Literary Supplement* would call the translation transatlantic.

Here, in recent translation, is an eminent Japanese author who liked English, and who, though a little too old to share in the craze for relative pronouns, had to cloud his sentences with clarifications: "It doesn't look as if he expects to live another ten or twenty years, as you seem to think he did." True, something could have been done to tidy up this particular translation, but even with the tenses in order, the fundamental problems would remain. The author was a great admirer of Meredith, and his characters frequently sound more like Victorians than like Japanese. "He doesn't seem to think he'll live another twenty years after all," we would say. But such is not the manner and style of the original.

And here is a promising young author who likes French: "It seemed to her as if it covered excesses of light and shadow with form, as if it were pulling together a dark passion without form, so to speak, with the bright, architectural will of music." What this says about a cloud—it is about a cloud—is uncertain. What it says about the author is this: he is enamored of French literature and French precision, and he is forced to work with unbending neo-Chinese nouns.

The character of their extraordinary language has surely had some effect on the character of the Japanese. It would be impertinent of a foreigner to say what, but one catches a hint in the behavior of novelists and critics. They first lament their poverty, which need not worry us. Compared to the poverty of serious writers in other countries, it is a fiction. Next, and more significantly, they lament their inability to have strong feelings of personal identity. Many of them seem to look upon their foggy, floating prose as in part responsible and are determined to change it. Henceforth

every act will have an actor, and everything a possessor, whatever
the cost.

"He showed his aunt to her room." A sentence that would not
strike one as particularly good or particularly bad English. Hardly
anyone would notice that it is half pronoun. But Japanese pronouns, as we have seen, are more obtrusive than English pronouns,
and the same sentence in Japanese becomes: "*Kare* wa *kare no* oba
wo *kanojo no* heya e" and so on. Japanese prose style tends to be
monotonous at best. It only approximates the spoken language,
and one of the literary conventions that remain has the effect of
ending almost every sentence with some form of the verb *to be,*
much as if every English sentence were to end "and that is a fact."
Add to this monotony the heavy monotony of pronouns or proto-
nouns that intrude as they never do in English, and the result is a
steady, Poe-like thumping.

If the revisionists are not deaf, they must think the sacrifice
worth making. It may one day lead to a new consciousness of the
individual, and the Japanese pronoun will then be as inoffensive as
the English pronoun is now. Only time will tell. For the present,
we must put up with pages of sentences beginning "that person
over there" and ending "now that is a fact." Perhaps we may be
forgiven for not trying to reproduce the full ease of the style in
English.

I have spoken of oh's and ah's, and of blubbering. They bring
us to the essential fact that Japanese is a very wordy language. Let
anyone who does not think so try reading one of the bracket-school
translations: he will find many sturdy workers in brackets, but he
will find innumerable drones wandering free. "Now that is a fact"
at the end of every sentence is one example; the remarkable number
of adverbs, the nearest English equivalent to which is "suddenly"
but which actually do not mean anything at all, is another.

Of the blubbering, much could be said. It calls up delicate
problems of emphasis and connotation. The Japanese are supposed
to be suspicious of the too overt emotion, but in their literature
they have been more tolerant of blubbering than the unbridled Oc-
cidentals even in their more Baroque moments. For over a thousand years, Japanese pillows and sleeves have been wet and not with
dew, and one often has trouble knowing whether the tears indicate
sorrow or pique or a willingness to play the game. They must be
translated with great tact. So must the sugar. "Your mother has a
beautiful soul" is likely to mean no more than "Your mother seems
very nice."

There are other matters on which the Japanese express themselves more openly than we are accustomed to: matters of evacuation, for instance. A bowdlerizer one may be when one has the hero relieve himself indoors rather than on Main Street, but the alternative is to shock when the original is not at all shocking. I was once accused of bowdlerizing because in a most intimate scene I changed a finger to a hand. I couldn't help it. The finger called up many memories of limericks, a heritage in which my author could not possibly have shared.

Of the problem that lies beneath all the other problems, a little has already been said, and only a little more can be said. English is largely the product of a religion which emphasizes individual responsibility, Japanese the product of a religion which, though it may be accommodated to many things, has on the whole produced resignation. Genji and his circle are perpetually sighing at their helplessness in the face of Karma. The result is that words, and especially verbs, carry wholly different moral connotations in the two languages. The Japanese verb that must be translated "to flee" or "to run away," for instance, is morally neutral as these dictionary equivalents are not. The hero of an autobiographical novel "flees" to the garden, let us say, because his wife is in labor and groaning without reserve; but when he chooses this verb he does not mean to be damning himself as a shirker. The likelihood is rather that he is reproving his wife for not getting the messy business over before tea. In English, however, he is shirking, whatever dictionary translation is chosen.

This may help explain why lady characters are usually more successful than gentlemen in Japanese novels. The moral tone added by translation and unconsciously read into the original by an Occidental can give the ladies a certain catlike charm. The gentlemen are only feckless.

Japanese, we may conclude, offers special difficulties in the application of Lord Woodhouselee's principles. The Japanese have a plaintive way of asking whether foreigners *really* understand their literature. To suggest that Japanese is, in a way, somewhat untranslatable is to invite a look compounded of pain and relief, the look of one hoping and yet fearing that the key has been found. Let us only say that there are difficulties, and that translation, as Allen Tate said of criticism, is forever impossible and forever necessary.